i.

Loans are
not returi
at the Libi
3 times. It
Please use

15 FE

10 MAP

29 D

13

25

1

Ch

The Well-Bred Person's
Book of Etiquette

The Well-Bred Person's Book of Etiquette

George Routledge

TEMPUS

First published 1891
Copyright © in this edition, Tempus Publishing, 2007

Tempus Publishing Limited
The Mill, Brimscombe Port,
Stroud, Gloucestershire, GL5 2QG
www.tempus-publishing.com

British Library Cataloguing in Publication Data.
A catalogue record for this book is available from the British Library.

ISBN 978 07524 4290 7

Typesetting and origination by Tempus Publishing Limited
Printed and bound in Great Britain

Contents

ETIQUETTE FOR LADIES

ETIQUETTE FOR GENTLEMEN

ETIQUETTE OF COURTSHIP AND MATRIMONY

HOW TO DRESS WELL.

I

INTRODUCTION

To introduce persons who are mutually unknown is to undertake a serious responsibility, and to certify to each the respectability of the other. Never undertake this responsibility without in the first place asking yourself whether the persons are likely to be agreeable to each other; nor, in the second place, without ascertaining whether it will be acceptable to both parties to become acquainted.

Always introduce the gentleman to the lady – never the lady to the gentleman. The chivalry of etiquette assumes that the lady is invariably the superior in right of her sex, and that the gentleman is honoured in the introduction. This rule is to be observed even when the social rank of the gentleman is higher than that of the lady.

Where the sexes are the same, always present the inferior to the superior.

Never present a gentleman to a lady without first asking her permission to do so.

When you are introduced to a gentleman, never offer your hand. When introduced, persons limit their recognition of each other to a bow. On the Continent, ladies never shake hands with gentlemen unless under circumstances of great intimacy.

Never introduce morning visitors who happen to encounter each other in your drawing-room, unless they are persons whom you have already obtained permission to make known to each other. Visitors thus casually meeting in the house of a friend should converse with ease and freedom, as if they were acquainted. That they are both friends of the hostess is a sufficient guarantee of their respectability. To be silent and stiff on such an occasion would show much ignorance and ill-breeding.

Persons who have met at the house of a mutual friend, without being introduced, should not bow if they afterwards meet elsewhere. A bow implies acquaintance; and persons who have not been introduced are not acquainted.

If you are walking with one friend, and presently meet with, or are joined by, a third, do not commit the too frequent error of introducing them to each other. You have even less right to do so than if they encountered each other at your house during a morning call.

There are some exceptions to the etiquette of introductions. At a ball, or evening party where there is dancing, the mistress of the house may introduce any gentleman to any lady without first asking the lady's permission. But she should first ascertain whether the lady is willing to dance; and this out of consideration for the gentleman, who may otherwise be refused. No man likes to be refused the hand of a lady, though it be only for a quadrille.

A sister may present her brother, or a mother her son, without any kind of preliminary; but only when there is no inferiority on the part of her own family to that of the acquaintance.

Friends may introduce friends at the house of a mutual acquaintance; but, as a rule, it is better to be introduced by the mistress of the house. Such an introduction carries more authority with it.

Introductions at evening parties are now almost wholly dispensed with. Persons who meet at a friend's house are ostensibly upon an equality, and pay a bad compliment to the host by appearing suspicious and formal. Some old-fashioned country hosts yet persevere in introducing each newcomer to all the assembled guests. It is a custom that cannot be too soon abolished, and one that places the last unfortunate visitor in a singularly awkward position. All that she can do is to make a semicircular courtesy, like a concert singer before an audience, and bear the general gaze with as much composure as possible.

If, when you enter a drawing-room, your name has been wrongly announced, or has passed unheard in the buzz of conversation, make your way at once to the mistress of the house, if you are a stranger, and introduce yourself by name. This should be done with the greatest simplicity, and your rank made as little of as possible.

An introduction given at a ball for the mere purpose of conducting a lady through a dance does not give the gentleman any right to bow to her on a future occasion. If he commits this error, she may remember that she is not bound to see, or return, his salutation.

II

LETTERS OF INTRODUCTION

Do not lightly give or promise letters of introduction. Always remember that when you give a letter of introduction you lay yourself under an obligation to the friend to whom it is addressed. If she lives in a great city, such as Paris or London, you in a measure compel her to undergo the penalty of escorting the stranger to some of those places of public entertainment in which the capital abounds. If your friend be a married lady, and the mistress of a house, you put her to the expense of inviting the stranger to her table. We cannot be too cautious how we tax the time and purse of a friend, or weigh too seriously the question of mutual advantage in the introduction. Always ask yourself whether the person introduced will be an acceptable acquaintance to the one to whom you present her; and whether the pleasure of knowing her will compensate for the time or money which it costs to entertain her. If the stranger is in any way unsuitable in habits or temperament, you inflict an annoyance on your friend instead of a pleasure. In questions of introduction never oblige one friend to the discomfort of another.

Those to whom letters of introduction have been given, should send them to the person to whom they are addressed, and enclose a card. Never deliver a letter of introduction in person. It places you in the most undignified position imaginable, and compels you to wait while it is being read, like a servant who has been told to wait for an answer. There is also another reason why you should not be yourself the bearer of your introduction; i.e., you compel the other person to receive you, whether she chooses or not. It may be that she is sufficiently ill-bred to take no notice of the letter when sent, and in such case, if you presented yourself with it, she would most probably receive you with rudeness. It is, at all events, more polite on your part to give her the option, and, perhaps, more pleasant. If the receiver of the letter be a really well-bred person, she will call upon you or leave her card the next day, and you should return her attentions within the week.

If, on the other hand, a stranger sends you a letter of introduction and her card, you are bound by the laws of politeness and hospitality, not only to call upon her the next day, but to follow up that attention with others. If you are in a position to do so, the most correct proceeding is to invite her to dine with you. Should this not be within your power, you can probably escort her to some of the exhibitions, bazaars, or concerts of the season; any of which would be interesting to a foreigner or provincial visitor. In short, etiquette demands that you shall exert yourself to show kindness to the stranger, if only out of compliment to the friend who introduced her to you.

If you invite her to dine with you, it is a better compliment to ask some others to meet her than to dine with her *tête-à-tête*. You are thereby giving her an opportunity of making other acquaintances, and are assisting your friend in still farther promoting the purpose for which she gave her the introduction to yourself.

Be careful at the same time only to ask such persons as she will feel are at least her own social equals.

A letter of introduction should be given unsealed, not alone because your friend may wish to know what you have said of her, but also as a guarantee of your own good faith. As you should never give such a letter unless you can speak highly of the bearer, this rule of etiquette is easy to observe. By requesting your friend to fasten the envelope before forwarding the letter to its destination, you tacitly give her permission to inspect its contents.

Let your note-paper be of the best quality and the proper size. Albert or Queen's size is the best for these purposes.

It has been well said that 'attention to the punctilios of politeness is a proof at once of self-respect, and of respect for your friend.' Though irksome at first, these trifles soon cease to be matters for memory, and become things of mere habit. To the thoroughly well-bred they are a second nature. Let no one neglect them who is desirous of pleasing in society; and, above all, let no one deem them unworthy of attention. They are precisely the trifles which do most to make social intercourse agreeable, and a knowledge of which distinguishes the gentlewoman from the *parvenue*.

III

VISITING, MORNING CALLS, CARDS

A morning visit should be paid between the hours of two and four p.m., in winter, and two and five in summer. By observing this rule you avoid intruding before the luncheon is removed, and leave in sufficient time to allow the lady of the house an hour or two of leisure for her dinner toilette.

Be careful always to avoid luncheon hours when you pay morning visits. Some ladies dine with their children at half-past one, and are consequently unprepared for the early reception of visitors. When you have once ascertained this to be the case, be careful never again to intrude at the same hour.

A good memory for these trifles is one of the hall-marks of good breeding.

Visits of ceremony should be short. If even the conversation should have become animated, beware of letting your call exceed half-an-hour's length. It is always better to let your friends regret than desire your withdrawal.

On returning visits of ceremony you may, without impoliteness, leave your card at the door without going in. Do not fail, however, to inquire if the family be well.

Should there be daughters or sisters residing with the lady upon whom you call, you may turn down a corner of your card, to signify that the visit is paid to all. It is in better taste, however, to leave cards for each.

Unless when returning thanks for 'kind inquiries', or announcing your arrival in, or departure from, town, it is not considered respectful to send round cards by a servant.

Leave-taking cards have P.P.C. (*pour prendre congé*) written in the corner. Some use P.D.A. (pour dire adieu).

It is not the fashion on the Continent for unmarried ladies to affix any equivalent to the English 'Miss' to their visiting cards. Emilie Dubois, or Kätchen Clauss, is thought more simple and elegant than if preceded by Mademoiselle or Fraülein. Some English girls have of late adopted this good custom, and it would be well if it became general.

Autographic facsimiles for visiting cards are affectations in any persons but those who are personally remarkable for talent, and whose autographs, or facsimiles of them, would be prized as curiosities. A card bearing the autographic signature of Agnes Strickland or Mary Somerville, though only a lithographic facsimile, would have a certain interest; whereas the signature of Jane Smith would be not only valueless, but would make the owner ridiculous.

Visits of condolence are paid within the week after the event which occasions them. Personal visits of this kind are made by relations and very intimate friends only. Acquaintances should leave cards with narrow mourning borders.

On the first occasion when you are received by the family after the death of one of its members, it is etiquette to wear slight mourning.

Umbrellas should invariably be left in the hall.

Never take favourite dogs into a drawing-room when you make a morning call. Their feet may be dusty, or they may bark at the sight of strangers, or, being of too friendly a disposition, may take the liberty of lying on a lady's gown, or jumping on the sofas and easy chairs. Where your friend has a favourite cat already established before the fire, a battle may ensue, and one or other of the pets be seriously hurt. Besides, many persons have a constitutional antipathy to dogs, and others never allow their own to be seen in the sitting-rooms. For all or any of these reasons, a visitor has no right to inflict upon her friend the society of her dog as well as of herself. Neither is it well for a mother to take young children with her when she pays morning visits; their presence, unless they are unusually well trained, can only be productive of anxiety to both yourself and your hostess. She, while striving to amuse them, or to appear interested in them, is secretly anxious for the fate of her album, or the ornaments on her *étagére*; while the mother is trembling lest her children should say or do something objectionable.

If other visitors are announced, and you have already remained as long as courtesy requires, wait till they are seated, and then rise from your chair, take leave of your hostess, and bow politely to the newly arrived guests. You will, perhaps, be urged to remain, but, having once risen, it is best to go. There is always a certain air of gaucherie in resuming your seat and repeating the ceremony of leave-taking.

If you have occasion to look at your watch during a call, ask permission to do so, and apologise for it on the plea of other appointments.

In receiving morning visitors, it is not necessary that the lady should lay aside the employment in which she may be engaged, particularly if it consists of light or ornamental needle-work. Politeness, however, requires that music, drawing, or any occupation which would completely engross the attention, be at once abandoned.

You need not advance to receive visitors when announced, unless they are persons to whom you are desirous of testifying particular attention. It is sufficient if a lady rises to receive her visitors, moves forward a single step to shake hands with them, and remains standing till they are seated.

When your visitors rise to take leave you should rise also, and remain standing till they have quite left the room. Do not accompany them to the door, but be careful to ring in good time, that the servant may be ready in the hall to let them out.

A lady should dress well, but not too richly, when she pays a morning visit. If she has a carriage at command, she may dress more elegantly than if she were on foot. The question of morning and afternoon dress will be found fully treated in Section VII.

IV

CONVERSATION

There is no conversation so graceful, so varied, so sparkling, as that of an intellectual and cultivated woman. Excellence in this particular is, indeed, one of the attributes of the sex, and should be cultivated by every gentlewoman who aspires to please in general society.

In order to talk well, three conditions are indisputable, namely tact, a good memory, and a fair education.

Remember that people take more interest in their own affairs than in anything else which you can name. If you wish your conversation to be thoroughly agreeable, lead a mother to talk of her children, a young lady of her last ball, an author of his forthcoming book, or an artist of his exhibition picture. Having furnished the topic, you need only listen; and you are sure to be thought not only agreeable, but thoroughly sensible and well-informed.

Be careful, however, on the other hand, not always to make a point of talking to persons upon general matters relating to their professions. To show an interest in their immediate concerns is flattering; but to converse with them too much about their own arts looks as if you thought them ignorant of other topics.

Remember in conversation that a voice 'gentle and low' is, above all other extraneous acquirements, 'an excellent thing in woman.' There is a certain distinct but subdued tone of voice which is peculiar to only well-bred persons. A loud voice is both disagreeable and vulgar. It is better to err by the use of too low than too loud a tone.

Remember that all 'slang' is vulgar. It has become of late unfortunately prevalent, and we know many ladies who pride themselves on the saucy chique with which they adopt certain Americanisms, and other cant phrases of the day. Such habits cannot be too severely reprehended. They lower the tone of society and the standard of thought. It is a great mistake to suppose that slang is in any way a substitute for wit.

The use of proverbs is equally vulgar in conversation; and puns, unless they rise to the rank of witticisms, are to be scrupulously avoided. A lady-punster is a most unpleasing phenomenon, and we would advise no young woman, however witty she may be, to cultivate this kind of verbal talent.

Long arguments in general company, however entertaining to the disputants, are tiresome to the last degree to all others. You should always endeavour to prevent the conversation from dwelling too long upon one topic.

Religion is a topic which should never be introduced in society. It is the one subject on which persons are most likely to differ, and least able to preserve temper.

Never interrupt a person who is speaking. It has been aptly said that 'if you interrupt a speaker in the middle of his sentence, you act almost as rudely as if, when walking with a companion, you were to thrust yourself before him, and stop his progress.'

To listen well is almost as great an art as to talk well. It is not enough only to listen. You must endeavour to seem interested in the conversation of others.

It is considered extremely ill-bred when two persons whisper in society, or converse in a language with which all present are not familiar. If you have private matters to discuss, you should appoint a proper time and place to do so, without paying others the ill compliment of excluding them from your conversation.

If a foreigner be one of the guests at a small party, and does not understand English sufficiently to follow what is said, good breeding demands that the conversation shall be carried on in his own language. If at a dinner-party, the same rule applies to those at his end of the table.

If upon the entrance of a visitor you carry on the thread of a previous conversation, you should briefly recapitulate to him what has been said before he arrived.

Do not be always witty, even though you should be so happily gifted as to need the caution. To outshine others on every occasion is the surest road to unpopularity.

Always look, but never stare, at those with whom you converse.

In order to meet the general needs of conversation in society, it is necessary that a gentlewoman should be acquainted with the current news and historical events of at least the last few years.

Never talk upon subjects of which you know nothing, unless it be for the purpose of acquiring information. Many young ladies imagine that because they play a little, sing a little, draw a little, and frequent exhibitions and operas, they are qualified judges of art. No mistake is more egregious or universal.

Those who introduce anecdotes into their conversation are warned that these should invariably be 'short, witty, eloquent, new, and not far-fetched.'

Scandal is the least excusable of all conversational vulgarities.

In conversing with a woman of rank, do not too frequently give her her title. Only a lady's maid interlards every sentence with 'My Lady,' or 'My Lord.' It is, however, well to show that you remember the station of your interlocutor by now and then introducing some such phrase as, 'I think I have already mentioned to your Grace' or, 'I believe, Madam, you were observing'.

A peer or baron may occasionally, as in an address, be styled 'My Lord,' but a lady of equal rank must only be addressed as 'Madam.' In general, however, a nobleman or lady of high rank should only be addressed as you would address any other gentleman or lady. The Prince of Wales himself is only styled 'Sir' in conversation, and the Queen 'Madam.'

V

NOTES OF INVITATION, &c

Notes of invitation and acceptance are written in the third person and the simplest style. The old-fashioned preliminary of 'presenting compliments' is discontinued by the most elegant letter writers.

All notes of invitation are now issued in the name of the mistress of the house only, as follows:

> Mrs. Norman requests the honour of Sir George and Lady Thurlow's company at an evening party, on Monday, 14th of June.

Others prefer the subjoined form, which is purchaseable ready printed upon either cards or note paper, with blanks for names or dates:

> Mrs. Norman,
> At home,
> Monday evening, June 14th inst.

An 'At home' is, however, considered somewhat less stately than an evening party, and partakes more of the character of a *conversazione*.

The reply to a note of invitation should be couched as follows:

> Mr. Berkeley has much pleasure in accepting Mrs. Norman's polite invitation for monday evening, june the 14th instant.

Never 'avail' yourself of an invitation. Above all, never speak or write of an invitation as 'an invite.' It is neither good breeding nor good English.

Notes of invitation and reply should be written on small paper of the best quality, and enclosed in envelopes to correspond.

Note paper of the most dainty and fastidious kind may be used by a lady with propriety and elegance, but only when she is writing to her friends and equals. Business letters or letters to her tradespeople should be written on plain paper, and enclosed either in an adhesive envelope, or sealed with red wax.

Never omit the address and date from any letter, whether of business or friendship.

Letters in the first person addressed to strangers should begin with 'Sir,' or 'Madam,' and end with 'I have the honour to be your very obedient servant.' Some object to this form of words from a mistaken sense of pride; but it is merely a form, and, rightly apprehended, evinces a 'proud humility,' which implies more condescension than a less formal phrase.

At the end of your letter, at some little distance below your signature, and in the left corner of your paper, write the name of the person to whom your letter is addressed; as 'Lady Dalhousie,' or 'Edward Munroe, Esquire.'

It is more polite to write Esquire at full length than to curtail it to Esq.

In writing to persons much your superior or inferior, use as few words as possible. In the former case, to take up much of a great man's time is to take a liberty; in the latter, to be diffuse is to be too familiar. It is only in familiar correspondence that long letters are permissible.

In writing to a tradesman, begin your letter by addressing him by name, as 'Mr. Jones, Sir.' A letter thus begun may, with propriety, be ended with 'Sir, yours truly.'

Letters to persons whom you meet frequently in society, without having arrived at intimacy, may commence with 'Dear Madam,' and end with 'I am, dear Madam, yours very truly.'

Letters commencing 'My dear Madam,' addressed to persons whom you appreciate, and with whom you are on friendly terms, may end with 'I am, my dear Madam, yours very faithfully,' or 'yours very sincerely.'

To be prompt in replying to a letter is to be polite.

Lady correspondents are too apt to over-emphasise in their letter-writing, and in general evince a sad disregard of the laws of punctuation. We would respectfully suggest that a comma is not designed to answer every purpose, and that the underlining of every second or third word adds nothing to the eloquence or clearness of a letter, however certain it may be to provoke an unflattering smile upon the lips of the reader.

All letters must be prepaid.

VI

THE PROMENADE

In England, a lady may accept the arm of a gentleman with whom she is walking, even though he be only an acquaintance. This is not the case either in America or on the Continent. There a lady can take the arm of no gentleman who is not either her husband, lover, or near relative.

If a lady has been making purchases during her walk, she may permit the gentleman who accompanies her to carry any small, parcel that she may have in her own hand; but she should not burthen him with more than one under any circumstances whatever.

Two ladies may without any impropriety take each one arm of a single cavalier; but one lady cannot, with either grace or the sanction of custom take the arms of two gentlemen at the same time.

When a lady is walking with a gentleman in a park, or public garden, or through the rooms of an exhibition, and becomes fatigued, it is the gentleman's duty to find her a seat. If, however, as is very frequently the case, he is himself obliged to remain standing, the lady should make a point of rising as soon as she is sufficiently rested, and not abuse either the patience or politeness of her companion.

It is the place of the lady to bow first, if she meets a gentleman of her acquaintance. When you meet friends or acquaintances in the streets, the exhibitions, or any public places, be careful not to pronounce their names so loudly as to attract the attention of bystanders. Never call across the street, or attempt to carry on a dialogue in a public vehicle, unless your interlocutor occupies the seat beside your own.

VII

DRESS

To dress well requires something more than a full purse and a pretty figure. It needs taste, good sense, and refinement. Dress may almost be classed as one of the fine arts. It is certainly one of those arts, the cultivation of which is indispensable to any person moving in the upper or middle classes of society. Very clever women are too frequently indifferent to the graces of the toilette; and women who wish to be thought clever affect indifference. In the one case it is an error, and in the other a folly. It is not enough that a gentlewoman should be clever, or well-educated, or well-born. To take her due place in society, she must be acquainted with all that this little book proposes to teach. She must, above all else, know how to enter a room, how to perform a graceful salutation, and how to dress. Of these three important qualifications, the most important, because the most observed, is the latter.

Let your style of dress always be appropriate to the hour of the day. To dress too finely in the morning, or to be seen in a morning dress in the evening, is equally vulgar and out of place.

Light and inexpensive materials are fittest for morning wear; dark silk dresses for the promenade or carriage; and low dresses of rich or transparent stuffs for the dinner and ball. A young lady cannot dress with too much simplicity in the early part of the day. A morning dress of some simple material, and delicate whole colour, with collar and cuffs of spotless linen, is, perhaps, the most becoming and elegant of morning toilettes.

Never dress very richly or showily in the street. It attracts attention of no enviable kind, and is looked upon as a want of good breeding. In the carriage a lady may dress as elegantly as she pleases.

With respect to ballroom toilette, its fashions are so variable, that statements which are true of it today, may be false a month hence. Respecting no institution of modern society is it so difficult to pronounce half-a-dozen permanent rules.

We may, perhaps, be permitted to suggest the following leading principles; but we do so with diffidence. Rich colours harmonise with rich brunette complexions and dark hair. Delicate colours are the most suitable for delicate and fragile styles of beauty. Very young ladies are never so suitably attired as in white. Ladies who dance should wear dresses of light and diaphanous materials, such as tulle, gauze, crape, net, &c., over coloured silk slips. Silk dresses are not suitable for dancing. A married lady who dances only a few quadrilles may wear a décolleté silk dress with propriety.

Very stout persons should never wear white. It has the effect of adding to the bulk of the figure.

Black and scarlet, or black and violet, are worn in mourning.

A lady in deep mourning should not dance at all.

However fashionable it may be to wear very long dresses, those ladies who go to a ball with the intention of dancing and enjoying the dance, should cause their dresses to be made short enough to clear the ground. We would ask them whether it is not better to accept this slight deviation from an absurd fashion, than to appear for three parts of the evening in a torn and pinned-up skirt?

Well-made shoes, whatever their colour or material, and faultless gloves, are indispensable to the effect of a ball-room toilette.

Much jewellery is out of place in a ball-room. Beautiful flowers, whether natural or artificial, are the loveliest ornaments that a lady can wear on these occasions.

At small dinner parties, low dresses are not so indispensable as they were held to be some years since. High dresses of transparent materials, and low bodices with capes of black lace, are considered sufficiently full dress on these occasions. At large dinners only the fullest dress is appropriate.

Very young ladies should wear but little jewellery. Pearls are deemed most appropriate for the young and unmarried.

Let your jewellery be always the best of its kind. Nothing is so vulgar, either in youth or age, as the use of false ornaments.

There is as much propriety to be observed in the wearing of jewellery as in the wearing of dresses. Diamonds, pearls, rubies, and all transparent precious stones belong to evening dress, and should on no account be worn before dinner. In the morning let your rings be of the more simple and massive kind; wear no bracelets; and limit your jewellery to a good brooch, gold chain, and watch. Your diamonds and pearls would be as much out of place during the morning as a low dress, or a wreath.

It is well to remember in the choice of jewellery that mere costliness is not always the test of value; and that an exquisite work of art, such as a fine cameo, or a natural rarity, such as a black pearl, is a more *distingué* possession than a large brilliant which any rich and tasteless vulgarian can buy as easily as yourself. Of all precious stones, the opal is one of the most lovely and least commonplace. No vulgar woman purchases an opal. She invariably prefers the more showy ruby, emerald, or sapphire.

A true gentlewoman is always faultlessly neat. No richness of toilette in the afternoon, no diamonds in the evening, can atone for unbrushed hair, a soiled collar, or untidy slippers at breakfast.

Never be seen in the street without gloves; and never let your gloves be of any material that is not kid or calf. Worsted or cotton gloves are unutterably vulgar. Your gloves should fit to the last degree of perfection.

In these days of public baths and universal progress, we trust that it is unnecessary to do more than hint at the necessity of the most fastidious personal cleanliness. The hair, the teeth, the nails, should be faultlessly kept; and a muslin dress that has been worn once too often, a dingy pocket-handkerchief, or a soiled pair of light gloves, are things to be scrupulously avoided by any young lady who is ambitious of preserving the exterior of a gentlewoman.

Remember that the make of your corsage is of even greater importance than the make of your dress. No dressmaker can fit you well, or make your bodices in the manner most becoming to your figure, if the corsage beneath be not of the best description.

Your boots and gloves should always be faultless.

Perfumes should be used only in the evening, and then in moderation. Let your perfumes be of the most delicate and *recherché* kind. Nothing is more vulgar than a coarse ordinary scent; and of all coarse, ordinary scents, the most objectionable are musk and patchouli.

Finally, every lady should remember that to dress well is a duty which she owes to society; but that to make it her idol is to commit something worse than a folly. Fashion is made for woman; not woman for fashion.

VIII

MORNING AND EVENING PARTIES

The morning party is a modern invention. It was unknown to our fathers and mothers, and even to ourselves till quite lately. A morning party is seldom given out of the season that is to say, during any months except those of May, June, and July. It begins about two o'clock and ends about five, and the entertainment consists for the most part of conversation, music, and (if there be a garden) croquet, lawn billiards, archery, &c. 'Aunt Sally' is now out of fashion. The refreshments are given in the form of a *déjeuner à la fourchette*.

Elegant morning dress, general good manners, and some acquaintance with the topics of the day and the games above named, are all the qualifications especially necessary to a lady at a morning party.

An evening party begins about nine o'clock p.m., and ends about midnight, or somewhat later. Good breeding neither demands that you should present yourself at the commencement, nor remain till the close of the evening. You come and go as may be most convenient to you, and by these means are at liberty, during the height of the season when evening parties are numerous, to present yourself at two or three houses during a single evening.

When your name is announced, look for the lady of the house, and pay your respects to her before you even seem to see any other of your friends who may be in the room. At very large and fashionable receptions, the hostess is generally to be found near the door. Should you, however, find yourself separated by a dense crowd of guests, you are at liberty to recognise those who are near you, and those whom you encounter as you make your way slowly through the throng.

General salutations of the company are now wholly disused. In society a lady only recognises her own friends and acquaintances.

If you are at the house of a new acquaintance and find yourself among entire strangers, remember that by so meeting under one roof you are all in a certain sense made known to one another, and should, therefore, converse freely, as equals. To shrink away to a side-table and affect to be absorbed in some album or illustrated work; or, if you find one unlucky acquaintance in the room, to fasten upon her like a drowning man clinging to a spar, are gaucheries which no shyness can excuse.

If you possess any musical accomplishments, do not wait to be pressed and entreated by your hostess, but comply immediately when she pays you the compliment of inviting you to play or sing. Remember, however, that only the lady of the house has the right to ask you. If others do so, you can put them off in some polite way; but must not comply till the hostess herself invites you.

Be scrupulous to observe silence when any of the company are playing or singing. Remember that they are doing this for the amusement of the rest; and that to talk at such a time is as ill-bred as if you were to turn your back upon a person who was talking to you, and begin a conversation with someone else.

If you are yourself the performer, bear in mind that in music, as in speech, 'brevity is the soul of wit.' Two verses of a song, or four pages of a piece, are at all times enough to give pleasure. If your audience desire more they will ask for more; and it is infinitely more flattering to be encored than to receive the thanks of your hearers, not so much in gratitude for what you have given them, but in relief that you have left off. You should try to suit your music, like your conversation, to your company. A solo of Beethoven's would be as much out of place in some circles as a comic song at a quakers' meeting. To those who only care for the light popularities of the season, give Balfe and Verdi, Glover and Julien. To connoisseurs, if you perform well enough to venture, give such music as will be likely to meet the exigencies of a fine taste. Above all, attempt nothing that you cannot execute with ease and precision.

If the party be of a small and social kind, and those games called by the French *les jeux innocents* are proposed, do not object to join in them when invited. It may be that they demand some slight exercise of wit and readiness, and that you do not feel yourself calculated to shine in them; but it is better to seem dull than disagreeable, and those who are obliging can always find some clever neighbour to assist them in the moment of need.

Impromptu charades are frequently organised at friendly parties. Unless you have really some talent for acting and some readiness of speech, you should remember that you only put others out and expose your own inability by taking part in these entertainments. Of course, if your help is really needed, and you would disoblige by refusing, you must do your best, and by doing it as quietly and coolly as possible, avoid being awkward or ridiculous.

Even though you may take no pleasure in cards, some knowledge of the etiquette and rules belonging to the games most in vogue is necessary to you in society. If a fourth hand is wanted at a rubber, or if the rest of the company sit down to a round game, you would be deemed guilty of an impoliteness if you refused to join.

The games most commonly played in society are whist, loo, vingt-et-un, and speculation.

Whist requires four players. A pack of cards being spread upon the table with their faces downwards, the four players draw for partners. Those who draw the two highest cards and those who draw the two lowest become partners. The lowest of all claims the deal.[A]

Married people should not play at the same table, unless where the party is so small that it cannot be avoided. This rule supposes nothing so disgraceful to any married couple as dishonest collusion; but persons who play regularly together cannot fail to know so much of each other's mode of acting, under given circumstances, that the chances no longer remain perfectly even in favour of their adversaries.

Never play for higher stakes than you can afford to lose without regret. Cards should be resorted to for amusement only; for excitement, never.

No well-bred person ever loses temper at the card-table. You have no right to sit down to the game unless you can bear a long run of ill-luck with perfect composure, and are prepared cheerfully to pass over any blunders that your partner may chance to make.

If you are an indifferent player, make a point of saying so before you join a party at whist. If the others are fine players they will be infinitely more obliged to you for declining than accepting their invitation. In any case you have no right to spoil their pleasure by your bad play.

Never let even politeness induce you to play for very high stakes. Etiquette is the minor morality of life; but it never should be allowed to outweigh the higher code of right and wrong.

Young ladies may decline to play at cards without being deemed guilty of impoliteness.

No very young lady should appear at an evening party without an escort.

In retiring from a crowded party it is unnecessary that you should seek out the hostess for the purpose of bidding her a formal goodnight. By doing this you would, perhaps, remind others that it was getting late, and cause the party to break up. If you meet the lady of the house on your way to the drawing-room door, take your leave of her as unobtrusively as possible, and slip away without attracting the attention of her other guests.

[Footnote A: For a succinct guide to whist, loo, vingt-et-un, speculation, &c., &c., &c., see Routledge's Card-player, by G.F. Pardon, price sixpence.]

IX

THE DINNER TABLE

To be acquainted with every detail of the etiquette pertaining to this subject is of the highest importance to every gentlewoman. Ease, *savoir faire*, and good breeding are nowhere more indispensable than at the dinner table, and the absence of them is nowhere more apparent. How to eat soup and what to do with a cherry-stone are weighty considerations when taken as the index of social status; and it is not too much to say, that a young woman who elected to take claret with her fish, or ate peas with her knife, would justly risk the punishment of being banished from good society. As this subject is one of the most important of which we have to treat, we may be pardoned for introducing an appropriate anecdote related by the French poet Delille: Delille and Marmontel were dining together in the month of April, 1786, and the conversation happened to turn upon dinner table customs. Marmontel observed how many little things a well-bred man was obliged to know, if he would avoid being ridiculous at the tables of his friends.

'They are, indeed, innumerable,' said Delille; 'and the most annoying fact of all is, that not all the wit and good sense in the world can help one to divine them untaught. A little while ago, for instance, the Abbé Cosson, who is Professor of Literature at the Collège Mazarin, was describing to me a grand dinner to which he had been invited at Versailles, and to which he had sat down in the company of peers, princes, and marshals of France.'

'I'll wager now,' said I, 'that you committed a hundred blunders in the etiquette of the table!'

'How so?' replied the Abbé, somewhat nettled. 'What blunders could I make? It seems to me that I did precisely as others did.'

'And I, on the contrary, would stake my life that you did nothing as others did. But let us begin at the beginning, and see which is right. In the first place there was your table napkin – what did you do with that when you sat down at table?

"What did I do with my table-napkin? Why, I did like the rest of the guests: I shook it out of the folds, spread it before me, and fastened one corner to my button-hole.'

'Very well, mon cher; you were the only person who did so. No one shakes, spreads, and fastens a table-napkin in that manner. You should have only laid it across your knees. What soup had you?

"Turtle.'

'And how did you eat it?

"Like every one else, I suppose. I took my spoon in one hand, and my fork in the other – '

'Your fork! Good heavens! None but a savage eats soup with a fork. But go on. What did you take next?

"A boiled egg.'

'Good; and what did you do with the shell?

"Not eat it, certainly. I left it, of course, in the egg-cup.'

'Without breaking it through with your spoon?

"Without breaking it.'

'Then, my dear fellow, permit me to tell you that no one eats an egg without breaking the shell and leaving the spoon standing in it. And after your egg?

"I asked for some *bouilli*.'

'For *bouilli*! It is a term that no one uses. You should have asked for beef – never for *bouilli*. Well, and after the *bouilli*?

"I asked the Abbé de Radonvilliers for some fowl.'

'Wretched man! Fowl, indeed! You should have asked for chicken or capon. The word 'fowl' is never heard out of the kitchen. But all this applies only to what you ate; tell me something of what you drank, and how you asked for it.

"I asked for champagne and bordeaux from those who had the bottles before them.'

'Know then, my good friend, that only a waiter, who has no time or breath to spare, asks for champagne or bordeaux. A gentleman asks for *vin de champagne* and *vin de bordeaux*. And now inform me how you ate your bread?

"Undoubtedly like all the rest of the world. I cut it into small square pieces with my knife.'

'Then let me tell you that no one cuts bread. You should always break it. Let us go on to the coffee. How did you drink yours?

"Pshaw! At least I could make no mistake in that. It was boiling hot, so I poured it, a little at a time, in the saucer, and drank it as it cooled.'

'*Eh bien*! then you assuredly acted as no other gentleman in the room. Nothing can be more vulgar than to pour tea or coffee into a saucer. You should have waited till it cooled, and then have drunk it from the cup. And now you see, my dear cousin, that so far from doing precisely as others did, you acted in no one respect according to the laws prescribed by etiquette.'

An invitation to dine should be replied to immediately, and unequivocally accepted or declined. Once accepted, nothing but an event of the last importance should cause you to fail in your engagement.

To be exactly punctual is the strictest politeness on these occasions. If you are too early, you are in the way; if too late, you spoil the dinner, annoy the hostess, and are hated by the rest of the guests. Some authorities are even of opinion that in the question of a dinner-party 'never' is better than 'late;' and one author has gone so far as to say, 'if you do not reach the house till dinner is served, you had better retire, and send an apology, and not interrupt the harmony of the courses by awkward excuses and cold acceptance.'

When the party is assembled, the mistress or master of the house will point out to each gentleman the lady whom he is to conduct to the table. The guests then go down according to precedence of rank. This order of precedence must be arranged by the host or hostess, as the guests are probably unacquainted, and cannot know each other's social rank.

When the society is of a distinguished kind the hostess will do well to consult Debrett or Burke, before arranging her visitors.

When rank is not in question, other claims to precedence must be considered. The lady who is the greatest stranger should be taken down by the master of the house, and the gentleman who is the greatest stranger should conduct the hostess. Married ladies take precedence of single ladies, elder ladies of younger ones, and so forth.

When dinner is announced, the host offers his arm to the lady of most distinction, invites the rest to follow by a few words or a bow, and leads the way. The lady of the house should then follow with the gentleman who is most entitled to that honour, and the visitors follow in the order that has been previously arranged. The lady of the house frequently remains, however, till the last, that she may see her guests go down in their prescribed order; but the plan is not a convenient one. It is much better that the hostess should be in her place as the guests enter the dining-room, in order that she may indicate their seats to them as they enter, and not find them all crowded together in uncertainty when she arrives.

The number of guests at a dinner-party should always be determined by the size of the table. When the party is too small, conversation flags, and a general air of desolation pervades the table. When they are too many, every one is inconvenienced. A space of two feet should be allowed to each person. It is well to arrange a party in such wise that the number of ladies and gentlemen be equal.

It requires some tact to distribute your guests so that each shall find himself with a neighbour to his taste; but as much of the success of a dinner will always depend on this matter, it is worth some consideration. If you have a wit, or a particularly good talker, among your visitors, it is well to place him near the centre of the table, where he can be heard and talked to by all. It is obviously a bad plan to place two such persons in close proximity. They extinguish each other. Neither is it advisable to assign two neighbouring seats to two gentlemen of the same profession, as they are likely to fall into exclusive conversation and amuse no one but themselves. A little consideration of the politics, religious opinions, and tastes of his friends, will enable a judicious host to avoid many quicksands, and establish much pleasant intercourse on the occasion of a dinner-party.

The lady of the house takes the head of the table. The gentleman who led her down to dinner occupies the seat on her right hand, and the gentleman next in order of precedence, that on her left. The master of the house takes the foot of the table. The lady whom he escorted sits on his right hand, and the lady next in order of precedence on his left.

As soon as you are seated at table, remove your gloves, place your table-napkin across your knees, and remove the roll which you find probably within it to the left side of your plate.

The soup should be placed on the table first. Some old-fashioned persons still place soup and fish together; but 'it is a custom more honoured in the breach than the observance.' Still more old-fashioned, and in still worse taste is it to ask your guests if they will take 'soup or fish.' They are as much separate courses as the fish and the meat; and all experienced diners take both. In any case, it is inhospitable to appear to force a choice upon a visitor, when that visitor, in all probability, will prefer to take his soup first and his fish afterwards. All well-ordered dinners begin with soup, whether in summer or winter. The lady of the house should help it, and send it round without asking each individual in turn. It is as much an understood thing as the bread beside each plate, and those who do not choose it are always at liberty to leave it untasted.

In eating soup, remember always to take it from the side of the spoon, and to make no sound in doing so.

If the servants do not go round with wine the gentlemen should help the ladies and themselves to sherry or sauterne immediately after the soup.

You should never ask for a second supply of either soup or fish; it delays the next course, and keeps the table waiting.

Never offer to 'assist' your neighbours to this or that dish. The word is inexpressibly vulgar – all the more vulgar for its affectation of elegance. 'Shall I send you some mutton?' or 'may I help you to grouse?' is better chosen and better bred.

As a general rule, it is better not to ask your guests if they will partake of the dishes; but to send the plates round, and let them accept or decline them as they please. At very large dinners it is sometimes customary to distribute little lists of the order of the dishes at intervals along the table. It must be confessed that this gives somewhat the air of a dinner at an hotel; but it has the advantage of enabling the visitors to select their fare, and, as 'forewarned is forearmed,' to keep a corner, as the children say, for their favourite dishes.

As soon as you are helped, begin to eat; or, if the viands are too hot for your palate, take up your knife and fork and appear to begin. To wait for others is now not only old-fashioned, but ill-bred.

Never offer to pass on the plate to which you have been helped. This is a still more vulgar piece of politeness, and belongs to the manners of a hundred years ago. The lady of the house who sends your plate to you is the best judge of precedence at her own table.

In helping soup, fish, or any other dish, remember that to overfill a plate is as bad as to supply it too scantily. Silver fish-knives will now always be met with at the best tables; but where there are none, a piece of crust should be taken in the left hand, and the fork in the right. There is no exception to this rule in eating fish.

We presume it is scarcely necessary to remind our fair reader that she is never, under any circumstances, to convey her knife to her mouth. Peas are eaten with the fork; tarts, curry, and puddings of all kinds with the spoon.

Always help fish with a fish-slice, and tart and puddings with a spoon, or, if necessary, a spoon and fork.

Asparagus must be helped with the asparagus-tongs.

In eating asparagus, it is well to observe what others do, and act accordingly. Some very well-bred people eat it with the fingers; others cut off the heads, and convey them to the mouth upon the fork. It would be difficult to say which is the more correct.

In eating stone fruit, such as cherries, damsons, &c., the same rule had better be observed. Some put the stones out from the mouth into a spoon, and so convey them to the plate. Others cover the lips with the hand, drop them unseen into the palm, and so deposit them on the side of the plate. In our own opinion, the last is the better way, as it effectually conceals the return of the stones, which is certainly the point of highest importance. Of one thing we may be sure, and that is, that they must never be dropped from the mouth to the plate.

In helping sauce, always pour it on the side of the plate.

If the servants do not go round with the wine (which is by far the best custom), the gentlemen at a dinner table should take upon themselves the office of helping those ladies who sit near them. Young ladies seldom drink more than three glasses of wine at dinner; but married ladies, professional ladies, and those accustomed to society and habits of affluence, will habitually take five or even six, whether in their own homes or at the tables of their friends.

The habit of taking wine with each other has almost wholly gone out of fashion. A gentleman may ask the lady whom he conducted down to dinner; or he may ask the lady of the house to take wine with him. But even these last remnants of the old custom are fast falling into disuse.

Unless you are a total abstainer, it is extremely uncivil to decline taking wine if you are invited to do so. In accepting, you have only to pour a little fresh wine into your glass, look at the person who invited you, bow slightly, and take a sip from the glass.

It is particularly ill-bred to empty your glass on these occasions.

Certain wines are taken with certain dishes, by old-established custom – as sherry, or sauterne, with soup and fish; hock and claret with roast meat; punch with turtle; champagne with whitebait; port with venison; port, or burgundy, with game; sparkling wines between the roast and the confectionery; madeira with sweets; port with cheese; and for dessert, port, tokay, madeira, sherry, and claret. Red wines should never be iced, even in summer. Claret and burgundy should always be slightly warmed; claret-cup and champagne-cup should, of course, be iced.

Instead of cooling their wines in the ice-pail, some hosts have of late years introduced clear ice upon the table, broken up in small lumps, to be put inside the glasses. This is an innovation that cannot be too strictly reprehended or too soon abolished. Melting ice can but weaken the quality and flavour of the wine. Those who desire to drink wine and water can ask for iced water if they choose; but it savours too much of economy on the part of a host to insinuate the ice inside the glasses of his guests when the wine could be more effectually iced outside the bottle.

A silver knife and fork should be placed to each guest at dessert.

It is wise never to partake of any dish without knowing of what ingredients it is composed. You can always ask the servant who hands it to you, and you thereby avoid all danger of having to commit the impoliteness of leaving it, and showing that you do not approve of it.

Never speak while you have anything in your mouth.

Be careful never to taste soups or puddings till you are sure they are sufficiently cool; as, by disregarding this caution, you may be compelled to swallow what is dangerously hot, or be driven to the unpardonable alternative of returning it to your plate.

When eating or drinking, avoid every kind of audible testimony to the facts.

Finger-glasses, containing water slightly warmed and perfumed, are placed to each person at dessert. In these you may dip the tips of your fingers, wiping them afterwards on your table-napkin. If the finger-glass and doyley are placed on your dessert-plate, you should immediately remove the doyley to the left of your plate, and place the finger-glass upon it. By these means you leave the right for the wine-glasses.

Be careful to know the shapes of the various kinds of wine-glasses commonly in use, in order that you may never put forward one for another. High and narrow, and very broad and shallow glasses, are used for champagne; large, goblet-shaped glasses for burgundy and claret; ordinary wine-glasses for sherry and madeira; green glasses for hock; and somewhat large, bell-shaped glasses, for port.

Port, sherry, and madeira, are decanted. Hocks and champagnes appear in their native bottles. Claret and burgundy are handed round in a claret-jug.

The servants leave the room when the dessert is on the table.

Coffee and liqueurs should be handed round when the dessert has been about a quarter of an hour on the table. After this, the ladies generally retire.

The lady of the house should never send away her plate, or appear to have done eating, till all her guests have finished.

If you should unfortunately overturn or break anything, do not apologise for it. You can show your regret in your face, but it is not well-bred to put it into words.

To abstain from taking the last piece on the dish, or the last glass of wine in the decanter, only because it is the last, is highly ill-bred. It implies a fear on your part that the vacancy cannot be supplied, and almost conveys an affront to your host.

To those ladies who have houses and servants at command, we have one or two remarks to offer. Every housekeeper should be acquainted with the routine of a dinner and the etiquette of a dinner table. No lady should be utterly dependent on the taste and judgment of her cook. Though she need not know how to dress a dish, she should be able to judge of it when served. The mistress of a house, in short, should be to her cook what a publisher is to his authors – that is to say, competent to form a judgment upon their works, though himself incapable of writing even a magazine article.

If you wish to give a good dinner, and do not know in what manner to set about it, you will do wisely to order it from Birch, Kühn, or any other first-rate restaurateur. By these means you ensure the best cookery and a faultless carte.

Bear in mind that it is your duty to entertain your friends in the best manner that your means permit. This is the least you can do to recompense them for the expenditure of time and money which they incur in accepting your invitation.

'To invite a friend to dinner,' says Brillat Savarin, 'is to become responsible for his happiness so long as he is under your roof.' Again:
'He who receives friends at his table, without having bestowed his personal supervision upon the repast placed before them, is unworthy to have friends.'

A dinner, to be excellent, need not consist of a great variety of dishes; but everything should be of the best, and the cookery should be perfect. That which should be cool should be cool as ice; that which should be hot should be smoking; the attendance should be rapid and noiseless; the guests well assorted; the wines of the best quality; the host attentive and courteous; the room well lighted; and the time punctual.

Every dinner should begin with soup, be followed by fish, and include some kind of game. 'The soup is to the dinner,' we are told by Grisnod de la Regnière, 'what the portico is to a building, or the overture to an opera.'

To this aphorism we may be permitted to add that a chasse of cognac or curaçoa at the close of the dinner is like the epilogue at the end of a comedy.

Never reprove or give directions to your servants before guests. If a dish is not placed precisely where you would have wished it to stand, or the order of a course is reversed, let the error pass unobserved by yourself, and you may depend that it will be unnoticed by others.

If you are a mother, you will be wise never to let your children make their appearance at dessert when you entertain friends at dinner. Children are out of place on these occasions. Your guests only tolerate them through politeness; their presence interrupts the genial flow of after-dinner conversation; and you may rely upon it that, with the exception of yourself, and perhaps your husband, there is not a person at the table who does not wish them in the nursery.

The duties of hostess at a dinner-party are not onerous; but they demand tact and good breeding, grace of bearing, and self-possession in no ordinary degree. She does not often carve. She has no active duties to perform; but she must neglect nothing, forget nothing, put all her guests at their ease, encourage the timid, draw out the silent, and pay every possible attention to the requirements of each and all around her. No accident must ruffle her temper. No disappointment must embarrass her. She must see her old china broken without a sigh, and her best glass shattered with a smile. In short, to quote the language of a clever contemporary, she must have 'the genius of tact to perceive, and the genius of finesse to execute; ease and frankness of manner; a knowledge of the world that nothing can surprise; a calmness of temper that nothing can disturb; and a kindness of disposition that can never be exhausted.'

X

THE BALL-ROOM

As the number of guests at a dinner-party is regulated by the size of the table, so should the number of invitations to a ball be limited by the proportions of the ball-room. A prudent hostess will always invite a few more guests than she really desires to entertain, in the certainty that there will be some deserters when the appointed evening comes round; but she will at the same time remember that to overcrowd her room is to spoil the pleasure of those who love dancing, and that a party of this kind when too numerously attended is as great a failure as one at which too few are present.

A room which is nearly square, yet a little longer than it is broad, will be found the most favourable for a ball. It admits of two quadrille parties, or two round dances, at the same time. In a perfectly square room this arrangement is not so practicable or pleasant. A very long and narrow room is obviously of the worst shape for the purpose of dancing, and is fit only for quadrilles and country dances.

The top of the ball-room is the part nearest the orchestra. In a private room, the top is where it would be if the room were a dining-room. It is generally at the farthest point from the door. Dancers should be careful to ascertain the top of the room before taking their places, as the top couples always lead the dances.

A good floor is of the last importance in a ball-room. In a private house, nothing can be better than a smooth, well-stretched holland, with the carpet beneath.

Abundance of light and free ventilation are indispensable to the spirits and comfort of the dancers.

Good music is as necessary to the prosperity of a ball as good wine to the excellence of a dinner. No hostess should tax her friends for this part of the entertainment. It is the most injudicious economy imaginable. Ladies who would prefer to dance are tied to the pianoforte; and as few amateurs have been trained in the art of playing dance music with that strict attention to time and accent which is absolutely necessary to the comfort of the dancers, a total and general discontent is sure to result. To play dance music thoroughly well is a branch of the art which requires considerable practice. It is as different from every other kind of playing as whale fishing is from fly fishing. Those who give private balls will do well ever to bear this in mind, and to provide skilled musicians for the evening. For a small party, a piano and cornopean make a very pleasant combination. Unless where several instruments are engaged, we do not recommend the introduction of the violin: although in some respects the finest of all solo instruments, it is apt to sound thin and shrill when employed on mere inexpressive dance tunes, and played by a mere dance player.

Invitations to a ball should be issued in the name of the lady of the house, and written on small note paper of the best quality. Elegant printed forms, some of them printed in gold or silver, are to be had at every stationer's by those who prefer them. The paper may be gilt-edged, but not coloured. The sealing-wax used should be of some delicate hue.

An invitation to a ball should be sent out at least ten days before the evening appointed. A fortnight, three weeks, and even a month may be allowed in the way of notice.

Not more than two or three days should be permitted to elapse before you reply to an invitation of this kind. The reply should always be addressed to the lady of the house, and should be couched in the same person as the invitation. The following are the forms generally in use:

Mrs. Molyneux requests the honour of Captain Hamilton's company at an evening party, on Monday, March the 11th instant. Dancing will begin at Nine o'clock. Thursday, March 1st.

Captain Hamilton has much pleasure in accepting Mrs. Molyneux's polite invitation for Monday evening, March the 11th instant. Friday, March 2nd.

The old form of 'presenting compliments' is now out of fashion.

The lady who gives a ball[A] should endeavour to secure an equal number of dancers of both sexes. Many private parties are spoiled by the preponderance of young ladies, some of whom never get partners at all, unless they dance with each other.

A room should in all cases be provided for the accommodation of the ladies. In this room there ought to be several looking-glasses; attendants to assist the fair visitors in the arrangement of their hair and dress; and some place in which the cloaks and shawls can be laid in order, and found at a moment's notice. It is well to affix tickets to the cloaks, giving a duplicate at the same time to each lady, as at the public theatres and concert-rooms. Needles and thread should also be at hand, to repair any little accident incurred in dancing.

Another room should be devoted to refreshments, and kept amply supplied with coffee, lemonade, ices, wine, and biscuits during the evening. Where this cannot be arranged, the refreshments should be handed round between the dances.

The question of supper is one which so entirely depends on the means of those who give a ball or evening party, that very little can be said upon it in a treatise of this description. Where money is no object, it is of course always preferable to have the whole supper, 'with all appliances and means to boot,' sent in from some first-rate house. It spares all trouble whether to the entertainers or their servants, and relieves the hostess of every anxiety. Where circumstances render such a course imprudent, we would only observe that a home-provided supper, however simple, should be good of its kind, and abundant in quantity. Dancers are generally hungry people, and feel themselves much aggrieved if the supply of sandwiches proves unequal to the demand. Great inconvenience is often experienced through the difficulty of procuring cabs at the close of an evening party. Gentlemen who have been dancing, and are unprepared for walking, object to go home on foot, or seek vehicles for their wives and daughters. Female servants who have been in attendance upon the visitors during a whole evening ought not to be sent out. If even men-servants are kept, they may find it difficult to procure as many cabs as are necessary. The best thing that the giver of a private ball can do under these circumstances, is to engage a policeman with a lanthorn to attend on the pavement during the evening, and to give notice during the morning at a neighbouring cab-stand, so as to ensure a sufficient number of vehicles at the time when they are likely to be required.

A ball generally begins about half-past nine or ten o'clock.

To attempt to dance without a knowledge of dancing is not only to make one's self ridiculous, but one's partner also. No lady has a right to place a partner in this absurd position. Never forget a ball-room engagement. To do so is to commit an unpardonable offence against good breeding.

On entering the ball-room, the visitor should at once seek the lady of the house, and pay her respects to her. Having done this, she may exchange salutations with such friends and acquaintances as may be in the room.

No lady should accept an invitation to dance from a gentleman to whom she has not been introduced. In case any gentleman should commit the error of so inviting her, she should not excuse herself on the plea of a previous engagement, or of fatigue, as to do so would imply that she did not herself attach due importance to the necessary ceremony of introduction. Her best reply would be to the effect that she would have much pleasure in accepting his invitation, if he would procure an introduction to her. This observation may be taken as applying only to public balls. At a private party the host and hostess are sufficient guarantees for the respectability of their guests; and although a gentleman would show a singular want of knowledge of the laws of society in acting as we have supposed, the lady who should reply to him as if he were merely an impertinent stranger in a public assembly-room would be implying an affront to her entertainers. The mere fact of being assembled together under the roof of a mutual friend is in itself a kind of general introduction of the guests to each other.

An introduction given for the mere purpose of enabling a lady and gentleman to go through a dance together does not constitute an acquaintanceship. The lady is at liberty to pass the gentleman in the park the next day without recognition.

It is not necessary that a lady should be acquainted with the steps, in order to walk gracefully and easily through a quadrille. An easy carriage and a knowledge of the figure is all that is requisite. A round dance, however, should on no account be attempted without a thorough knowledge of the steps, and some previous practice.

No person who has not a good ear for time and tune need hope to dance well.

No lady should accept refreshments from a stranger at a public ball; for she would thereby lay herself under a pecuniary obligation. For these she must rely on her father, brothers, or old friends.

Good taste forbids that a lady should dance too frequently with the same partner at either a public or private ball.

Engaged persons should be careful not to commit this conspicuous solecism.

Engagements for one dance should not be made while the present dance is yet in progress.

Never attempt to take a place in a dance which has been previously engaged.

Withdraw from a private ball-room as quietly as possible, so that your departure may not be observed by others, and cause the party to break up. If you meet the lady of the house on your way out, take your leave of her in such a manner that her other guests may not suppose you are doing so; but do not seek her out for that purpose.

Never be seen without gloves in a ball-room, though it were for only a few moments. Ladies who dance much and are particularly *soigné* in matters relating to the toilette, take a second pair of gloves to replace the first when soiled.

A thoughtful hostess will never introduce a bad dancer to a good one, because she has no right to punish one friend in order to oblige another.

It is not customary for married persons to dance together in society.[B]

[Footnote A: It will be understood that we use the word 'ball' to signify a private party, where there is dancing, as well as a public ball.]

[Footnote B: For a more detailed account of the laws and business of the ball, see the chapter entitled 'The Ball-room Guide.']

XI

STAYING AT A FRIEND'S HOUSE: BREAKFAST, LUNCHEON, &c

A visitor is bound by the laws of social intercourse to conform in all respects to the habits of the house. In order to do this effectually, she should inquire, or cause her personal servant to inquire, what those habits are. To keep your friend's breakfast on the table till a late hour; to delay the dinner by want of punctuality; to accept other invitations, and treat his house as if it were merely an hotel to be slept in; or to keep the family up till unwonted hours, are alike evidences of a want of good feeling and good breeding.

At breakfast and lunch absolute punctuality is not imperative; but a visitor should avoid being always the last to appear at table.

No order of precedence is observed at either breakfast or luncheon. Persons take their seats as they come in, and, having exchanged their morning salutations, begin to eat without waiting for the rest of the party.

If letters are delivered to you at breakfast or luncheon, you may read them by asking permission from the lady who presides at the urn.

Always hold yourself at the disposal of those in whose house you are visiting. If they propose to ride, drive, walk, or otherwise occupy the day, you may take it for granted that these plans are made with reference to your enjoyment. You should, therefore, receive them with cheerfulness, enter into them with alacrity, and do your best to seem pleased, and be pleased, by the efforts which your friends make to entertain you.

You should never take a book from the library to your own room without requesting permission to borrow it. When it is lent, you should take every care that it sustains no injury while in your possession, and should cover it, if necessary.

A guest should endeavour to amuse herself as much as possible, and not be continually dependent on her hosts for entertainment. She should remember that, however welcome she may be, she is not always wanted.

Those who receive 'staying visitors,' as they are called, should remember that the truest hospitality is that which places the visitor most at her ease, and affords her the greatest opportunity for enjoyment. They should also remember that different persons have different ideas on the subject of enjoyment, and that the surest way of making a guest happy is to find out what gives her pleasure; not to impose that upon her which is pleasure to themselves.

A visitor should avoid giving unnecessary trouble to the servants of the house, and should be liberal to them on leaving.

The signal for retiring to rest is generally given by the appearance of the servant with wine, water, and biscuits, where a late dinner-hour is observed and suppers are not the custom. This is the last refreshment of the evening, and the visitor will do well to rise and wish good-night shortly after it has been partaken of by the family.

XII

GENERAL HINTS

Do not frequently repeat the name of the person with whom you are conversing. It implies either the extreme of hauteur or familiarity. We have already cautioned you against the repetition of titles. Deference can always be better expressed in the voice, manner, and countenance than in any forms of words.

Never speak of absent persons by only their Christian or surnames; but always as Mr. — or Mrs. —. Above all, never name anybody by the first letter of his name. Married people are sometimes guilty of this flagrant offence against taste.

No lady should permit any gentleman who is not a near relative, or very old friend of her family, to defray the cost of her entrance fee to any theatre or exhibition, or to pay for her refreshments or vehicles when she happens to be out under his protection.

If a person of greater age or higher rank than yourself desires you to step first into a carriage, or through a door, it is more polite to bow and obey than to decline.

Compliance with, and deference to, the wishes of others is the finest breeding.

When you cannot agree with the propositions advanced in general conversation, be silent. If pressed for your opinion, give it with modesty. Never defend your own views too warmly. When you find others remain unconvinced, drop the subject, or lead to some other topic.

Look at those who address you.

Never boast of your birth, your money, your grand friends, or anything that is yours. If you have travelled, do not introduce that information into your conversation at every opportunity. Anyone can travel with money and leisure. The real distinction is to come home with enlarged views, improved tastes, and a mind free from prejudice.

If you present a book to a friend, do not write his or her name in it, unless requested. You have no right to presume that it will be rendered any the more valuable for that addition; and you ought not to conclude beforehand that your gift will be accepted.

Never undervalue the gift which you are yourself offering; you have no business to offer it if it is valueless. Neither say that you do not want it yourself, or that you should throw it away if it were not accepted, &c., &c. Such apologies would be insults if true, and mean nothing if false.

No compliment that bears insincerity on the face of it is a compliment at all.

Unmarried ladies may not accept presents from gentlemen who are neither related nor engaged to them. Presents made by a married lady to a gentleman can only be offered in the joint names of her husband and herself.

Married ladies may occasionally accept presents from gentlemen who visit frequently at their houses, and who desire to show their sense of the hospitality which they receive there.

There is an art and propriety in the giving of presents which it requires a natural delicacy of disposition rightly to apprehend. You must not give too rich a gift, nor too poor a gift. You must not give to one much wealthier than yourself; and you must beware how you give to one much poorer, lest you offend her pride. You must never make a present with any expectation of a return; and you must not be too eager to make a return yourself, when you accept one. A gift must not be ostentatious, but it should be worth offering. On the other hand, mere costliness does not constitute the soul of a present.

A gift should be precious for something better than its price. It may have been brought by the giver from some far or famous place; it may be unique in its workmanship; it may be valuable only from association with some great man or strange event. Autographic papers, foreign curiosities, and the like, are elegant gifts. An author may offer his book, or a painter a sketch, with grace and propriety. Offerings of flowers and game are unexceptionable, and may be made even to those whose position is superior to that of the giver.

Never refuse a present unless under very exceptional circumstances. However humble the giver, and however poor the gift, you should appreciate the goodwill and intention, and accept it with kindness and thanks. Never say 'I fear I rob you,' or 'I am really ashamed to take it,' &c., &c. Such deprecatory phrases imply that you think the bestower of the gift cannot spare or afford it.

Acknowledge the receipt of a present without delay.

Give a foreigner his name in full, as Monsieur de Vigny – never as Monsieur only. In speaking of him, give him his title, if he has one. Foreign noblemen are addressed viva voce as Monsieur. In speaking of a foreign nobleman before his face, say Monsieur le Comte, or Monsieur le Marquis. In his absence, say Monsieur le Comte de Vigny.

Converse with a foreigner in his own language. If not competent to do so, apologise, and beg permission to speak English.

To get in and out of a carriage gracefully is a simple but important accomplishment. If there is but one step, and you are going to take your seat facing the horses, put your left foot on the step, and enter the carriage with your right, in such a manner as to drop at once into your seat. If you are about to sit with your back to the horses, reverse the process. As you step into the carriage, be careful to keep your back towards the seat you are about to occupy, so as to avoid the awkwardness of turning when you are once in.

Members of one family should not converse together in society.

Etiquette for Gentlemen

I

INTRODUCTION

To introduce persons who are mutually unknown is to undertake a serious responsibility, and to certify to each the respectability of the other. Never undertake this responsibility without in the first place asking yourself whether the persons are likely to be agreeable to each other; nor, in the second place, without ascertaining whether it will be acceptable to both parties to become acquainted.

Always introduce the gentleman to the lady – never the lady to the gentleman. The chivalry of etiquette assumes that the lady is invariably the superior in right of her sex, and that the gentleman is honoured in the introduction. This rule is to be observed even when the social rank of the gentleman is higher than that of the lady.

Where the sexes are the same, always present the inferior to the superior.

Never present a gentleman to a lady without first asking her permission to do so.

When you are introduced to a lady, never offer your hand. When introduced, persons limit their recognition of each other to a bow. On the Continent, ladies never shake hands with gentlemen unless under circumstances of great intimacy.

Never introduce morning visitors who happen to encounter each other in your rooms, unless they are persons whom you have already obtained permission to make known to each other. Visitors thus casually meeting in the house of a friend should converse with ease and freedom, as if they were acquainted. That they are both friends of the hostess is a sufficient guarantee of their respectability. To be silent and stiff on such an occasion would show much ignorance and ill-breeding.

Persons who have met at the house of a mutual friend without being introduced should not bow if they afterwards meet elsewhere. A bow implies acquaintance; and persons who have not been introduced are not acquainted.

If you are walking with one friend, and presently meet with, or are joined by, a third, do not commit the too frequent error of introducing them to each other. You have even less right to do so than if they encountered each other at your house during a morning call.

There are some exceptions to the etiquette of introductions. At a ball, or evening party where there is dancing, the mistress of the house may introduce any gentleman to any lady without first asking the lady's permission. But she should first ascertain whether the lady is willing to dance; and this out of consideration for the gentleman, who may otherwise be refused. No man likes to be refused the hand of a lady, though it be only for a quadrille.

A brother may present his sister, or a father his son, without any kind of preliminary; but only when there is no inferiority on the part of his own family to that of the acquaintance.

Friends may introduce friends at the house of a mutual acquaintance; but, as a rule, it is better to be introduced by the mistress of the house. Such an introduction carries more authority with it.

Introductions at evening parties are now almost wholly dispensed with. Persons who meet at a friend's house are ostensibly upon an equality, and pay a bad compliment to the host by appearing suspicious and formal. Some old-fashioned country hosts yet persevere in introducing each newcomer to all the assembled guests. It is a custom that cannot be too soon abolished, and one that places the last unfortunate visitor in a singularly awkward position. All that he can do is to make a semicircular bow, like a concert singer before an audience, and bear the general gaze with as much composure as possible.

If, when you enter a drawing-room, your name has been wrongly announced, or has passed unheard in the buzz of conversation, make your way at once to the mistress of the house, if you are a stranger, and introduce yourself by name. This should be done with the greatest simplicity, and your professional or titular rank made as little of as possible.

An introduction given at a ball for the mere purpose of conducting a lady through a dance does not give the gentleman any right to bow to her on a future occasion. If he commits this error, he must remember that she is not bound to see, or return, his salutation.

II

LETTERS OF INTRODUCTION

Do not lightly give or promise letters of introduction. Always remember that when you give a letter of introduction you lay yourself under an obligation to the friend to whom it is addressed. If he lives in a great city, such as Paris or London, you in a measure compel him to undergo the penalty of escorting the stranger to some of those places of public entertainment in which the capital abounds. In any case, you put him to the expense of inviting the stranger to his table. We cannot be too cautious how we tax the time and purse of a friend, or weigh too seriously the question of mutual advantage in the introduction. Always ask yourself whether the person introduced will be an acceptable acquaintance to the one to whom you present him; and whether the pleasure of knowing him will compensate for the time or money which it costs to entertain him. If the stranger is in any way unsuitable in habits or temperament, you inflict an annoyance on your friend instead of a pleasure. In questions of introduction never oblige one friend to the discomfort of another.

Those to whom letters of introduction have been given should send them to the person to whom they are addressed, and enclose a card. Never deliver a letter of introduction in person. It places you in the most undignified position imaginable, and compels you to wait while it is being read, like a footman who has been told to wait for an answer. There is also another reason why you should not be yourself the bearer of your introduction; i.e., you compel the other person to receive you, whether he chooses or not. It may be that he is sufficiently ill-bred to take no notice of the letter when sent, and in such case, if you presented yourself with it, he would most probably receive you with rudeness. It is, at all events, more polite on your part to give him the option, and perhaps more pleasant. If the receiver of the letter be a really well-bred person, he will call upon you or leave his card the next day, and you should return his attentions within the week.

If, on the other hand, a stranger sends you a letter of introduction and his card, you are bound by the laws of politeness and hospitality, not only to call upon him the next day, but to follow up that attention with others. If you are in a position to do so, the most correct proceeding is to invite him to dine with you. Should this not be within your power, you have probably the *entrée* to some private collections, clubhouses, theatres, or reading-rooms, and could devote a few hours to showing him these places. If you are but a clerk in a bank, remember that only to go over the Bank of England would be interesting to a foreigner or provincial visitor. In short, etiquette demands that you shall exert yourself to show kindness to the stranger, if only out of compliment to the friend who introduced him to you.

If you invite him to dine with you, it is a better compliment to ask some others to meet him, than to dine with him *tête-à-tête*. You are thereby giving him an opportunity of making other acquaintances, and are assisting your friend in still further promoting the purpose for which he gave him the introduction to yourself.

Be careful at the same time only to ask such persons as he will feel are at least his own social equals.

A letter of introduction should be given unsealed, not alone because your friend may wish to know what you have said of him, but also as a guarantee of your own good faith. As you should never give such a letter unless you can speak highly of the bearer, this rule of etiquette is easy to observe. By requesting your friend to fasten the envelope before forwarding the letter to its destination, you tacitly give him permission to inspect its contents.

Let your note paper be of the best quality and the proper size. Albert or Queen's size is the best for these purposes.

It has been well said that 'attention to the punctilios of politeness is a proof at once of self-respect, and of respect for your friend.' Though irksome at first, these trifles soon cease to be matters for memory, and become things of mere habit. To the thoroughly well-bred, they are a second nature. Let no one neglect them who is desirous of pleasing in society; and, above all, let no one deem them unworthy of a wise man's attention. They are precisely the trifles which do most to make social intercourse agreeable, and a knowledge of which distinguishes the gentleman from the boor.

III

VISITING, MORNING CALLS, CARDS

A morning visit should be paid between the hours of two and four p.m., in winter, and two and five in summer. By observing this rule you avoid intruding before the luncheon is removed, and leave in sufficient time to allow the lady of the house an hour or two of leisure for her dinner toilette.

Be careful always to avoid luncheon hours when you pay morning visits. Some ladies dine with their children at half-past one, and are consequently unprepared for the early reception of visitors. When you have once ascertained this to be the case, be careful never again to intrude at the same hour.

A good memory for these trifles is one of the hall-marks of good breeding.

Visits of ceremony should be short. If even the conversation should have become animated, beware of letting your call exceed half-an-hour's length. It is always better to let your friends regret than desire your withdrawal.

On returning visits of ceremony you may, without impoliteness, leave your card at the door without going in. Do not fail, however, to inquire if the family be well.

Should there be daughters or sisters residing with the lady upon whom you call, you may turn down a corner of your card, to signify that the visit is paid to all. It is in better taste, however, to leave cards for each.

Unless when returning thanks for 'kind inquiries,' or announcing your arrival in, or departure from, town, it is not considered respectful to send round cards by a servant.

Leave-taking cards have P.P.C. (pour prendre congé) written in the corner. Some use P.D.A. (pour dire adieu).

It is not the fashion on the Continent for gentlemen to affix Monsieur to their cards, Jules Achard, or Paolo Beni, looks more simple and elegant than if preceded by Monsieur, or Monsieur le Comte. Some English gentlemen have adopted this good custom, and it would be well if it became general.

Autographic facsimiles for visiting cards are affectations in any persons but those who are personally remarkable for talent and whose autographs, or facsimiles of them, would be prized as curiosities. A card bearing the autographic signature of Charles Dickens or George Cruikshank, though only a lithographic facsimile, would have a certain interest; whereas the signature of John Smith would be not only valueless, but would make the owner ridiculous.

The visiting cards of gentlemen are half the size of those used by ladies.

Visits of condolence are paid within the week after the event which occasions them. Personal visits of this kind are made by relations and very intimate friends only. Acquaintances should leave cards with narrow mourning borders.

On the first occasion when you are received by the family after the death of one of its members, it is etiquette to wear slight mourning.

When a gentleman makes a morning call, he should never leave his hat or riding-whip in the hall, but should take both into the room. To do otherwise would be to make himself too much at home. The hat, however, must never be laid on a table, piano, or any article of furniture; it should be held gracefully in the hand. If you are compelled to lay it aside, put it on the floor.

Umbrellas should invariably be left in the hall.

Never take favourite dogs into a drawing-room when you make a morning call. Their feet may be dusty, or they may bark at the sight of strangers, or, being of too friendly a disposition, may take the liberty of lying on a lady's gown, or jumping on the sofas and easy chairs. Where your friend has a favourite cat already established before the fire, a battle may ensue, and one or other of the pets be seriously hurt. Besides, many persons have a constitutional antipathy to dogs, and others never allow their own to be seen in the sitting-rooms. For all or any of these reasons, a visitor has no right to inflict upon his friend the society of his dog as well as of himself.

If, when you call upon a lady, you meet a lady visitor in her drawing-room, you should rise when that lady takes her leave, and escort her to her carriage, taking care, however, to return again to the drawing-room, though it be only for a few minutes, before taking your own leave. Not to do this would give you the appearance of accompanying the lady visitor; or might, at all events, look as if the society of your hostess were insufficient to entertain you when her friend had departed.

If other visitors are announced, and you have already remained as long as courtesy requires, wait till they are seated, and then rise from your chair, take leave of your hostess, and bow politely to the newly arrived guests. You will, perhaps, be urged to remain, but, having once risen, it is always best to go. There is always a certain air of gaucherie in resuming your seat and repeating the ceremony of leave-taking.

If you have occasion to look at your watch during a call, ask permission to do so, and apologise for it on the plea of other appointments.

IV

CONVERSATION

Let your conversation be adapted as skilfully as may be to your company. Some men make a point of talking commonplaces to all ladies alike, as if a woman could only be a trifler. Others, on the contrary, seem to forget in what respects the education of a lady differs from that of a gentleman, and commit the opposite error of conversing on topics with which ladies are seldom acquainted. A woman of sense has as much right to be annoyed by the one, as a lady of ordinary education by the other. You cannot pay a finer compliment to a woman of refinement and esprit than by leading the conversation into such a channel as may mark your appreciation of her superior attainments.

In talking with ladies of ordinary education, avoid political, scientific, or commercial topics, and choose only such subjects as are likely to be of interest to them.

Remember that people take more interest in their own affairs than in anything else which you can name. If you wish your conversation to be thoroughly agreeable, lead a mother to talk of her children, a young lady of her last ball, an author of his forthcoming book, or an artist of his exhibition picture. Having furnished the topic, you need only listen; and you are sure to be thought not only agreeable, but thoroughly sensible and well-informed.

Be careful, however, on the other hand, not always to make a point of talking to persons upon general matters relating to their professions. To show an interest in their immediate concerns is flattering; but to converse with them too much about their own arts looks as if you thought them ignorant of other topics.

Do not use a classical quotation in the presence of ladies without apologising for, or translating it. Even this should only be done when no other phrase would so aptly express your meaning. Whether in the presence of ladies or gentlemen, much display of learning is pedantic and out of place.

There is a certain distinct but subdued tone of voice which is peculiar to only well-bred persons. A loud voice is both disagreeable and vulgar. It is better to err by the use of too low than too loud a tone.

Remember that all 'slang' is vulgar. It has become of late unfortunately prevalent, and we have known even ladies pride themselves on the saucy chique with which they adopt certain Americanisms, and other cant phrases of the day.

Such habits cannot be too severely reprehended. They lower the tone of society and the standard of thought. It is a great mistake to suppose that slang is in any way a substitute for wit.

The use of proverbs is equally vulgar in conversation; and puns, unless they rise to the rank of witticisms, are to be scrupulously avoided. There is no greater nuisance in society than a dull and persevering punster.

Long arguments in general company, however entertaining to the disputants, are tiresome to the last degree to all others. You should always endeavour to prevent the conversation from dwelling too long upon one topic.

Religion is a topic which should never be introduced in society. It is the one subject on which persons are most likely to differ, and least able to preserve temper.

Never interrupt a person who is speaking. It has been aptly said that 'if you interrupt a speaker in the middle of his sentence, you act almost as rudely as if, when walking with a companion, you were to thrust yourself before him, and stop his progress.'

To listen well, is almost as great an art as to talk well. It is not enough only to listen. You must endeavour to seem interested in the conversation of others.

It is considered extremely ill-bred when two persons whisper in society, or converse in a language with which all present are not familiar. If you have private matters to discuss, you should appoint a proper time and place to do so, without paying others the ill compliment of excluding them from your conversation.

If a foreigner be one of the guests at a small party, and does not understand English sufficiently to follow what is said, good-breeding demands that conversation shall be carried on in his own language. If at a dinner-party, the same rule applies to those at his end of the table.

If upon the entrance of a visitor you carry on the thread of a previous conversation, you should briefly recapitulate to him what has been said before he arrived.

Do not be always witty, even though you should be so happily gifted as to need the caution. To outshine others on every occasion is the surest road to unpopularity.

Always look, but never stare, at those with whom you converse.

In order to meet the general needs of conversation in society, it is necessary that a man should be well acquainted with the current news and historical events of at least the last few years.

Never talk upon subjects of which you know nothing, unless it be for the purpose of acquiring information. Many young men imagine that because they frequent exhibitions and operas they are qualified judges of art. No mistake is more egregious or universal.

Those who introduce anecdotes into their conversation are warned that these should invariably be 'short, witty, eloquent, new, and not far-fetched.'

Scandal is the least excusable of all conversational vulgarities.

In conversing with a man of rank, do not too frequently give him his title. Only a servant interlards every sentence with 'my Lord,' or 'my Lady.' It is, however, well to show that you remember his station by now and then introducing some such phrase as – 'I think I have already mentioned to your Lordship' – or, 'I believe your Grace was observing'… In general, however, you should address a nobleman as you would any other gentleman. The Prince of Wales himself is only addressed as 'Sir,' in conversation, and the Queen as 'Madam.'

V

NOTES OF INVITATION, &c

Notes of invitation and acceptance are written in the third person and the simplest style. The old-fashioned preliminary of 'presenting compliments' is discontinued by the most elegant letter-writers.

All notes of invitation are now issued in the name of the mistress of the house only, as follows:

> Mrs. Norman requests the honour of Sir George and Lady Thurlow's company at an evening party, on Monday, 14th of June.

Others prefer the subjoined form, which is purchaseable ready printed upon either cards or note-paper, with blanks for names or dates:

> Mrs. Norman,
> At home,
> Monday evening, June 14th inst.

An 'At home' is, however, considered somewhat less stately than an evening party, and partakes more of the character of a *conversazione*.

The reply to a note of invitation should be couched as follows:

> Mr. Berkeley has much pleasure in accepting Mrs. Norman's polite invitation for Monday evening, June the 14th inst.

Never 'avail' yourself of an invitation. Above all, never speak or write of an invitation as 'an invite.' It is neither good breeding nor good English.

Notes of invitation and reply should be written on small paper of the best quality, and enclosed in envelopes to correspond.

A gentleman should never use sealing-wax of any colour but red, nor paper of any hue but white. Fancy papers, fantastic borders, dainty coloured wax, and the like elegant follies, are only admissible in the desk of a lady.

Never omit the address and date from any letter, whether of business, friendship, or ceremony.

Letters in the first person, addressed to strangers, should begin with 'Sir,' or 'Madam,' and end with 'I have the honour to be your very obedient servant.' Some object to this form of words from a mistaken sense of pride; but it is merely a form, and, rightly apprehended, evinces a 'proud humility,' which implies more condescension than a less formal phrase.

At the end of your letter, at some little distance below your signature, and in the left corner of your paper, write the name of the person to whom your letter is addressed; as 'Sir James Dalhousie,' or 'Edward Munroe, Esquire.'

It is more polite to write Esquire at full length than to curtail it to Esq.

In writing to persons much your superior or inferior, use as few words as possible. In the former case, to take up much of a great man's time is to take a liberty; in the latter to be diffuse is to be too familiar. It is only in familiar correspondence that long letters are permissible.

In writing to a tradesman, begin your letter by addressing him by name, as

Mr. Jones, Sir.

A letter thus begun may, with propriety, be ended with

Sir, yours truly.

Letters to persons whom you meet frequently in society, without having arrived at intimacy, may commence with 'Dear Sir,' and end with 'I am, dear Sir, yours very truly.'

Letters commencing 'My dear Sir,' addressed to persons whom you appreciate, and with whom you are on friendly terms, may end with 'I am, my dear Sir, yours very faithfully,' or 'yours very sincerely.'

To be prompt in replying to a letter is to be polite.

VI

THE PROMENADE

A well-bred man must entertain no respect for the brim of his hat. 'A bow,' says La Fontaine, 'is a note drawn at sight.' You are bound to acknowledge it immediately, and to the full amount. The two most elegant men of their day, Charles II and George IV, never failed to take off their hats to the meanest of their subjects. Always bear this example in mind; and remember that to nod, or merely to touch the brim of the hat, is far from courteous. True politeness demands that the hat should be quite lifted from the head.

On meeting friends with whom you are likely to shake hands, remove your hat with the left hand in order to leave the right hand free.

If you meet a lady in the street whom you are sufficiently intimate to address, do not stop her, but turn round and walk beside her in whichever direction she is going. When you have said all that you wish to say, you can take your leave.

If you meet a lady with whom you are not particularly well acquainted, wait for her recognition before you venture to bow to her.

In bowing to a lady whom you are not going to address, lift your hat with that hand which is farthest from her. For instance, if you pass her on the right side, use your left hand; if on the left, use your right.

If you are on horseback and wish to converse with a lady who is on foot, you must dismount and lead your horse, so as not to give her the fatigue of looking up to your level. Neither should you subject her to the impropriety of carrying on a conversation in a tone necessarily louder than is sanctioned in public by the laws of good breeding.

When you meet friends or acquaintances in the streets, the exhibitions, or any public places, take care not to pronounce their names so loudly as to attract the attention of the passers-by. Never call across the street: and never carry on a dialogue in a public vehicle, unless your interlocutor occupies the seat beside your own.

In walking with a lady, take charge of any small parcel, parasol, or book with which she may be encumbered.

If you so far forget what is elegant as to smoke in the street, at least never omit to fling away your cigar if you speak to a lady.

VII

DRESS

A great French writer has said, with as much grace as philosophy, that the artist and man of letters needs only a black coat and the absence of all pretension to place him on the level of the best society. It must be observed, however, that this remark applies only to the intellectual workers, who, if they do occasionally commit a minor solecism in dress or manners, are forgiven on account of their fame and talents. Other individuals are compelled to study what we have elsewhere called the 'by-laws of society;' and it would be well if artists and men of letters would more frequently do the same. It is not enough that a man should be clever, or well educated, or well born; to take his place in society he must be acquainted with all that this little book proposes to teach. He must, above all else, know how to enter the room, how to bow, and how to dress. Of these three indispensable qualifications, the most important, because the most observed, is the latter.

A gentleman should always be so well dressed that his dress shall never be observed at all. Does this sound like an enigma? It is not meant for one. It only implies that perfect simplicity is perfect elegance, and that the true test of taste in the toilette of a gentleman is its entire harmony, unobtrusiveness and becomingness. If any friend should say to you, 'What a handsome waistcoat you have on!' you may depend that a less handsome waistcoat would be in better taste. If you hear it said that Mr. So-and-So wears superb jewellery, you may conclude beforehand that he wears too much. Display, in short, is ever to be avoided, especially in matters of dress. The toilette is the domain of the fair sex. Let a wise man leave its graces and luxuries to his wife, daughters or sisters, and seek to be himself appreciated for something of higher worth than the embroidery upon his shirt front, or the trinkets on his chain.

To be too much in the fashion is as vulgar as to be too far behind it. No really well-bred man follows every new cut that he sees in his tailor's fashion-book. Only very young men, and those not of the most aristocratic circles, are guilty of this folly.

The author of *Pelham* has aptly said that a gentleman's coat should not fit too well. There is great truth and subtlety in this observation. To be fitted too well is to look like a tailor's assistant. This is the great fault which we have to find in the style of even the best bred Frenchmen. They look as if they had just stepped out of a fashion-book, and lack the careless ease which makes an English gentleman look as if his clothes belonged to him, and not he to his clothes.

In the morning wear frock coats, double-breasted waistcoats, and trousers of light or dark colours, according to the season.

In the evening, though only in the bosom of your own family, wear only black, and be as scrupulous to put on a dress coat as if you expected visitors. If you have sons, bring them up to do the same. It is the observance of these minor trifles in domestic etiquette which marks the true gentleman.

For evening parties, dinner parties, and balls, wear a black dress coat, black trousers, black silk or cloth waistcoat, white cravat, white or grey kid gloves, and thin patent leather boots. A black cravat may be worn in full dress, but is not so elegant as a white one. A black velvet waistcoat should only be worn at a dinner party.

Let your jewellery be of the best, but the least gaudy description, and wear it very sparingly. A set of good studs, a gold watch and guard, and one handsome ring, are as many ornaments as a gentleman can wear with propriety. In the morning let your ring be a seal ring, with your crest or arms engraved upon it. In the evening it may be a diamond. Your studs, however valuable, should be small.

It is well to remember in the choice of jewellery that mere costliness is not always the test of value; and that an exquisite work of art, such as a fine cameo, or a natural rarity, such as a black pearl, is a more *distingué* possession than a large brilliant which any rich and tasteless vulgarian can buy as easily as yourself. For a ring, the gentleman of fine taste would prefer a precious antique intaglio to the handsomest diamond or ruby that could be brought at Hunt and Roskell's. The most elegant gentleman with whom the author was ever acquainted – a man familiar with all the Courts of Europe – never wore any other shirt-studs in full dress than three valuable black pearls, each about the size of a pea, and by no means beautiful to look at.

Of all precious stones, the opal is one of the most lovely and the least common-place. No vulgar man purchases an opal. He invariably prefers the more showy diamond, ruby, sapphire, or emerald.

Unless you are a snuff-taker, never carry any but a white pocket-handkerchief.

If in the morning you wear a long cravat fastened by a pin, be careful to avoid what may be called alliteration of colour. We have seen a turquoise pin worn in a violet-coloured cravat, and the effect was frightful. Choose, if possible, complementary colours, and their secondaries. For instance, if the stone in your pin be a turquoise, wear it with brown, or crimson mixed with black, or black and orange. If a ruby, contrast it with shades of green. The same rule holds good with regard to the mixture and contrast of colours in your waistcoat or cravat. Thus, a buff waistcoat and a blue tie, or brown and blue, or brown and green, or brown and magenta, green and magenta, green and mauve, are all good arrangements of colour.

Very light coloured cloths for morning wear are to be avoided, even in the height of summer; and fancy cloths of strange patterns and mixtures are exceedingly objectionable.

Coloured shirts may be worn in the morning; but they should be small in pattern, and quiet in colour.

With a coloured shirt, always wear a white collar.

Never wear a cap, unless in the fields or garden; and let your hat be always black.

For a gentleman's wedding dress see the 'Etiquette of Courtship and Matrimony.'

If your sight compels you to wear spectacles, let them be of the best and lightest make, and mounted in gold or blue steel.

If you suffer from weak sight, and are obliged to wear coloured glasses, let them be of blue or smoke colour. Green are detestable.

Never be seen in the street without gloves; and never let your gloves be of any material that is not kid or calf. Worsted or cotton gloves are unutterably vulgar. Your gloves should fit to the last degree of perfection.

In these days of public baths and universal progress, we trust that it is unnecessary to do more than hint at the necessity of the most fastidious personal cleanliness. The hair, the teeth, the nails, should be faultlessly kept; and a soiled shirt, a dingy pocket-handkerchief, or a light waistcoat that has been worn once too often, are things to be scrupulously avoided by any man who is ambitious of preserving the exterior of a gentleman.

VIII

RIDING AND DRIVING

In riding, as in walking, give the lady the wall.

If you assist a lady to mount, hold your hand at a convenient distance from the ground, that she may place her foot in it. As she springs, you aid her by the impetus of your hand.

In doing this, it is always better to agree upon a signal, that her spring and your assistance may come at the same moment.

For this purpose there is no better form than the old duelling one of 'one, two, three.'

When the lady is in the saddle, it is your place to find the stirrup for her, and guide her left foot to it. When this is done, she rises in her seat and you assist her to draw her habit straight.

Even when a groom is present, it is more polite for the gentleman himself to perform this office for his fair companion; as it would be more polite for him to hand her a chair than to have it handed by a servant.

If the lady be light, you must take care not to give her too much impetus in mounting. We have known a lady nearly thrown over her horse by a misplaced zeal of this kind.

In riding with a lady, never permit her to pay the tolls.

If a gate has to be opened, we need hardly observe that it is your place to hold it open till the lady has passed through.

In driving, a gentleman places himself with his back to the horses, and leaves the best seat for the ladies.

If you are alone in a carriage with a lady, never sit beside her, unless you are her husband, father, son, or brother. Even though you be her affianced lover, you should still observe this rule of etiquette. To do otherwise, would be to assume the unceremonious air of a husband.

When the carriage stops, the gentleman should alight first, in order to assist the lady.

To get in and out of a carriage gracefully is a simple but important accomplishment. If there is but one step, and you are going to take your seat facing the horses, put your left foot on the step and enter the carriage with your right in such a manner as to drop at once into your seat. If you are about to sit with your back to the horses, reverse the process. As you step into the carriage, be careful to keep your back towards the seat you are about to occupy, so as to avoid the awkwardness of turning when you are once in.

A gentleman cannot be too careful to avoid stepping on ladies' dresses when he gets in or out of a carriage. He should also beware of shutting them in with the door.

IX

MORNING AND EVENING PARTIES

The morning party is a modern invention; it was unknown to our fathers and mothers, and even to ourselves, till quite lately. A morning party is seldom given out of the season – that is to say, during any months except those of May, June, and July. It begins about two o'clock and ends about five, and the entertainment consists for the most part of conversation, music, and (if there be a garden) croquet, lawn billiards, archery, &c. 'Aunt Sally' is now out of fashion. The refreshments are given in the form of a *déjeûner à la fourchette*.

Elegant morning dress, general good manners, and some acquaintance with the topics of the day and the games above named, are all the qualifications especially necessary to a gentleman at a morning party.

An evening party begins about nine o'clock, p.m., and ends about midnight, or somewhat later. Good breeding neither demands that you should present yourself at the commencement, nor remain till the close of the evening. You come and go as may be most convenient to you, and by these means are at liberty, during the height of the season when evening parties are numerous, to present yourself at two or three houses during a single evening.

Always put your gloves on before entering the drawing-room, and be careful that there is no speck of mud upon your boots or trousers.

General salutations of the company are now wholly disused. In society, a man only recognises his own friends and acquaintances.

If you are at the house of a new acquaintance and find yourself among entire strangers, remember that by so meeting under one roof you are all in a certain sense made known to one another, and should therefore converse freely, as equals. To shrink away to a side-table and affect to be absorbed in some album or illustrated work; or, if you find one unlucky acquaintance in the room, to fasten upon him like a drowning man clinging to a spar, are gaucheries which no shyness can excuse. An easy and unembarrassed manner, and the self-possession requisite to open a conversation with those who happen to be near you, are the indispensable credentials of a well-bred man.

At an evening party, do not remain too long in one spot. To be afraid to move from one drawing-room to another is the sure sign of a neophyte in society.

If you have occasion to use your handkerchief, do so as noiselessly as possible. To blow your nose as if it were a trombone, or to turn your head aside when using your handkerchief, are vulgarities scrupulously to be avoided.

Never stand upon the hearth-rug with your back to the fire, either in a friend's house or your own. We have seen even well-bred men at evening parties commit this selfish and vulgar solecism.

Never offer anyone the chair from which you have just risen, unless there be no other disengaged.

If when supper is announced no lady has been especially placed under your care by the hostess, offer your arm to whichever lady you may have last conversed with.

If you possess any musical accomplishments, do not wait to be pressed and entreated by your hostess, but comply immediately when she pays you the compliment of inviting you to play or sing. Remember, however, that only the lady of the house has the right to ask you. If others do so, you can put them off in some polite way; but must not comply till the hostess herself invites you.

If you sing comic songs, be careful that they are of the most unexceptionable kind, and likely to offend neither the tastes nor prejudices of the society in which you find yourself. At an evening party given expressly in honour of a distinguished lady of colour, we once heard a thoughtless amateur dash into the broadly comic, but terribly appropriate nigger song of 'Sally come up.' Before he had got through the first verse, he had perceived his mistake, and was so overwhelmed with shame that he could scarcely preserve sufficient presence of mind to carry him through to the end.

If the party be of a small and social kind, and those games called by the French *les jeux innocents* are proposed, do not object to join in them when invited. It may be that they demand some slight exercise of wit and readiness, and that you do not feel yourself calculated to shine in them; but it is better to seem dull than disagreeable, and those who are obliging can always find some clever neighbour to assist them in the moment of need. The game of 'consequences' is one which unfortunately gives too much scope to liberty of expression. If you join in this game, we cannot too earnestly enjoin you never to write down one word which the most pure-minded woman present might not read aloud without a blush. Jests of an equivocal character are not only vulgar, but contemptible.

Impromptu charades are frequently organised at friendly parties. Unless you have really some talent for acting and some readiness of speech, you should remember that you only put others out and expose your own inability by taking part in these entertainments. Of course, if your help is really needed and you would disoblige by refusing, you must do your best, and by doing it as quietly and coolly as possible, avoid being awkward or ridiculous.

Should an impromptu polka or quadrille be got up after supper at a party where no dancing was intended, be sure not to omit putting on gloves before you stand up. It is well always to have a pair of white gloves in your pocket in case of need; but even black are better under these circumstances than none.

Even though you may take no pleasure in cards, some knowledge of the etiquette and rules belonging to the games most in vogue is necessary to you in society. If a fourth hand is wanted at a rubber, or if the rest of the company sit down to a round game, you would be deemed guilty of an impoliteness if you refused to join.

The games most commonly played in society are whist, loo, vingt-et-un, and speculation.

Whist requires four players.[A] A pack of cards being spread upon the table with their faces downwards, the four players draw for partners. Those who draw the two highest cards and those who draw the two lowest become partners. The lowest of all claims the deal.

Married people should not play at the same table, unless where the party is so small that it cannot be avoided. This rule supposes nothing so disgraceful to any married couple as dishonest collusion; but persons who play regularly together cannot fail to know so much of each other's mode of acting, under given circumstances, that the chances no longer remain perfectly even in favour of their adversaries.

Never play for higher stakes than you can afford to lose without regret. Cards should be resorted to for amusement only; for excitement, never.

No well-bred person ever loses temper at the card-table. You have no right to sit down to the game unless you can bear a long run of ill luck with perfect composure, and are prepared cheerfully to pass over any blunders that your partner may chance to make.

If you are an indifferent player, make a point of saying so before you join a party at whist. If the others are fine players they will be infinitely more obliged to you for declining than accepting their invitation. In any case you have no right to spoil their pleasure by your bad play.

Never let even politeness induce you to play for very high stakes. Etiquette is the minor morality of life; but it never should be allowed to outweigh the higher code of right and wrong.

Be scrupulous to observe silence when any of the company are playing or singing. Remember that they are doing this for the amusement of the rest; and that to talk at such a time is as ill-bred as if you were to turn your back upon a person who was talking to you, and begin a conversation with some one else.

If you are yourself the performer, bear in mind that in music, as in speech, 'brevity is the soul of wit.' Two verses of a song, or four pages of a piece, are at all times enough to give pleasure. If your audience desire more they will ask for more; and it is infinitely more flattering to be encored than to receive the thanks of your hearers, not so much in gratitude for what you have given them, but in relief that you have left off. You should try to suit your music, like your conversation, to your company. A solo of Beethoven's would be as much out of place in some circles as a comic song at a Quakers' meeting. To those who only care for the light popularities, of the season, give Balfe and Verdi, Glover and Jullien. To connoisseurs, if you perform well enough to venture, give such music as will be likely to meet the exigencies of a fine taste. Above all, attempt nothing that you cannot execute with ease and precision.

In retiring from a crowded party it is unnecessary that you should seek out the hostess for the purpose of bidding her a formal good night. By doing this you would, perhaps, remind others that it was getting late, and cause the party to break up.

If you meet the lady of the house on your way to the drawing-room door, take your leave of her as unobtrusively as possible, and slip away without attracting the attention of her other guests.

[Footnote A: For a succinct guide to whist, loo, vingt-et-un, speculation, &c., &c., &c., see Routledge's Card-player,' by G.F. Pardon, price sixpence.]

X

THE DINNER TABLE

To be acquainted with every detail of the etiquette pertaining to this subject is of the highest importance to every gentleman. Ease, *savoir faire*, and good breeding are nowhere more indispensable than at the dinner table, and the absence of them are nowhere more apparent. How to eat soup and what to do with a cherry-stone are weighty considerations when taken as the index of social status; and it is not too much to say, that a man who elected to take claret with his fish, or ate peas with his knife, would justly risk the punishment of being banished from good society. As this subject is one of the most important of which we have to treat, we may be pardoned for introducing an appropriate anecdote related by the French poet Delille: Delille and Marmontel were dining together in the month of April, 1786, and the conversation happened to turn upon dinner table customs. Marmontel observed how many little things a well-bred man was obliged to know, if he would avoid being ridiculous at the tables of his friends:

'They are, indeed, innumerable,' said Delille; 'and the most annoying fact of all is, that not all the wit and good sense in the world can help one to divine them untaught. A little while ago, for instance, the Abbé Cosson, who is Professor of Literature at the Collège Mazarin, was describing to me a grand dinner to which he had been invited at Versailles, and to which he had sat down in the company of peers, princes, and marshals of France.'
'I'll wager now,' said I, 'that you committed a hundred blunders in the etiquette of the table!'

'How so?' replied the Abbé, somewhat nettled. 'What blunders could I make? It seems to me that I did precisely as others did.'

'And I, on the contrary, would stake my life that you did nothing as others did. But let us begin at the beginning, and see which is right. In the first place there was your table napkin – what did you do with that when you sat down at table?

"What did I do with my table-napkin? Why, I did like the rest of the guests: I shook it out of the folds, spread it before me, and fastened one corner to my button-hole.'

'Very well, mon cher; you were the only person who did so. No one shakes, spreads, and fastens a table-napkin in that manner. You should have only laid it across your knees. What soup had you?

"Turtle.'

'And how did you eat it?

"Like every one else, I suppose. I took my spoon in one hand, and my fork in the other – '

'Your fork! Good heavens! None but a savage eats soup with a fork. But go on. What did you take next?

"A boiled egg.'

'Good; and what did you do with the shell?

'Not eat it, certainly. I left it, of course, in the egg-cup.'

'Without breaking it through with your spoon?

"Without breaking it.'

'Then, my dear fellow, permit me to tell you that no one eats an egg without breaking the shell and leaving the spoon standing in it. And after your egg?

"I asked for some *bouilli*.'

'For *bouilli*! It is a term that no one uses. You should have asked for beef – never for *bouilli*. Well, and after the *bouilli*?

"I asked the Abbé de Radonvilliers for some fowl.'

'Wretched man! Fowl, indeed! You should have asked for chicken or capon. The word 'fowl' is never heard out of the kitchen. But all this applies only to what you ate; tell me something of what you drank, and how you asked for it.

"I asked for champagne and bordeaux from those who had the bottles before them.'

Know then, my good friend, that only a waiter, who has no time or breath to spare, asks for champagne or bordeaux. A gentleman asks for *vin de champagne* and *vin de bordeaux*. And now inform me how you ate your bread?

"Undoubtedly like all the rest of the world. I cut it into small square pieces with my knife.'

'Then let me tell you that no one cuts bread. You should always break it. Let us go on to the coffee. How did you drink yours?

"Pshaw! At least I could make no mistake in that. It was boiling hot, so I poured it, a little at a time, in the saucer, and drank it as it cooled.'

'*Eh bien*! then you assuredly acted as no other gentleman in the room. Nothing can be more vulgar than to pour tea or coffee into a saucer. You should have waited till it cooled, and then have drunk it from the cup. And now you see, my dear cousin, that so far from doing precisely as others did, you acted in no one respect according to the laws prescribed by etiquette.'

An invitation to dine should be replied to immediately, and unequivocally accepted or declined. Once accepted, nothing but an event of the last importance should cause you to fail in your engagement.

To be exactly punctual is the strictest politeness on these occasions. If you are too early, you are in the way; if too late, you spoil the dinner, annoy the hostess, and are hated by the rest of the guests. Some authorities are even of opinion that in the question of a dinner-party 'never' is better than 'late;' and one author has gone so far as to say, if you do not reach the house till dinner is served, you had better retire to a restaurateur's, and thence send an apology, and not interrupt the harmony of the courses by awkward excuses and cold acceptance.

When the party is assembled, the mistress or master of the house will point out to each gentleman the lady whom he is to conduct to the table. If she be a stranger, you had better seek an introduction; if a previous acquaintance, take care to be near her when the dinner is announced, offer your arm, and go down according to precedence of rank. This order of precedence must be arranged by the host or hostess, as the guests are probably unacquainted, and cannot know each other's social rank.

When the society is of a distinguished kind, the host will do well to consult Debrett or Burke, before arranging his visitors.

When rank is not in question, other claims to precedence must be considered. The lady who is the greatest stranger should be taken down by the master of the house, and the gentleman who is the greatest stranger should conduct the hostess. Married ladies take precedence of single ladies, elder ladies of younger ones, and so forth.

When dinner is announced, the host offers his arm to the lady of most distinction, invites the rest to follow by a few words or a bow, and leads the way. The lady of the house should then follow with the gentleman who is most entitled to that honour, and the visitors follow in the order that the master of the house has previously arranged. The lady of the house frequently remains, however, till the last, that she may see her guests go down in their prescribed order; but the plan is not a convenient one. It is much better that the hostess should be in her place as the guests enter the dining-room, in order that she may indicate their seats to them as they come in, and not find them all crowded together in uncertainty when she arrives.

The number of guests at a dinner-party should always be determined by the size of the table. When the party is too small, conversation flags, and a general air of desolation pervades the table. When they are too many, everyone is inconvenienced. A space of two feet should be allowed to each person. It is well to arrange a party in such wise that the number of ladies and gentlemen be equal.

It requires some tact to distribute your guests so that each shall find himself with a neighbour to his taste; but as much of the success of a dinner will always depend on this matter, it is worth some consideration. If you have a wit, or a particularly good talker, among your visitors, it is well to place him near the centre of the table, where he can be heard and talked to by all. It is obviously a bad plan to place two such persons in close proximity. They extinguish each other. Neither is it advisable to assign two neighbouring seats to two gentlemen of the same profession, as they are likely to fall into exclusive conversation and amuse no one but themselves. A little consideration of the politics, religious opinions, and tastes of his friends, will enable a judicious host to avoid many quicksands, and establish much pleasant intercourse on the occasion of a dinner party.

The lady of the house takes the head of the table. The gentleman who led her down to dinner occupies the seat on her right hand, and the gentleman next in order of precedence, that on her left. The master of the house takes the foot of the table. The lady whom he escorted sits on his right hand, and the lady next in order of precedence on his left.

The gentlemen who support the lady of the house should offer to relieve her of the duties of hostess. Many ladies are well pleased thus to delegate the difficulties of carving, and all gentlemen who accept invitations to dinner should be prepared to render such assistance when called upon. To offer to carve a dish, and then perform the office unskilfully, is an unpardonable gaucherie. Every gentleman should carve, and carve well.

As soon as you are seated at the table, remove your gloves, place your table napkin across your knees, and remove the roll which you find probably within it to the left side of your plate.

The soup should be placed on the table first. Some old-fashioned persons still place soup and fish together; but 'it is a custom more honoured in the breach than the observance.' Still more old-fashioned, and in still worse taste is it to ask your guests if they will take 'soup or fish.' They are as much separate courses as the fish and the meat; and all experienced diners take both. In any case, it is inhospitable to appear to force a choice upon a visitor, when that visitor, in all probability, will prefer to take his soup first and his fish afterwards. All well-ordered dinners begin with soup, whether in summer or winter. The lady of the house should help it and send it round, without asking each individual in turn. It is as much an understood thing as the bread beside each plate, and those who do not choose it, are always at liberty to leave it untasted.

In eating soup, remember always to take it from the side of the spoon, and to make no sound in doing so.

If the servants do not go round with wine the gentlemen should help the ladies and themselves to sherry or sauterne immediately after the soup.

You should never ask for a second supply of either soup or fish; it delays the next course, and keeps the table waiting.

Never offer to 'assist' your neighbours to this or that dish. The word is inexpressibly vulgar – all the more vulgar for its affectation of elegance. 'Shall I send you some mutton?' or 'may I help you to grouse?' is better chosen and better bred.

As a general rule, it is better not to ask your guests if they will partake of the dishes; but to send the plates round, and let them accept or decline them as they please. At very large dinners it is sometimes customary to distribute little lists of the order of the dishes at intervals along the table. It must be confessed that this gives somewhat the air of a dinner at an hotel; but it has the advantage of enabling the visitors to select their fare, and, as 'forewarned is forearmed,' to keep a corner, as the children say, for their favourite dishes.

If you are asked to take wine, it is polite to select the same as that which your interlocutor is drinking. If you invite a lady to take wine, you should ask her which she will prefer, and then take the same yourself. Should you, however, for any reason prefer some other vintage, you can take it by courteously requesting her permission.

As soon as you are helped, begin to eat; or, if the viands are too hot for your palate, take up your knife and fork and appear to begin. To wait for others is now not only old-fashioned, but ill-bred.

Never offer to pass on the plate to which you have been helped. This is a still more vulgar piece of politeness, and belongs to the manners of a hundred years ago. The lady of the house who sends your plate to you is the best judge of precedence at her own table.

In helping soup, fish, or any other dish, remember that to overfill a plate is as bad as to supply it too scantily.

Silver fish-knives will now always be met with at the best tables; but where there are none, a piece of crust should be taken in the left hand, and the fork in the right. There is no exception to this rule in eating fish.

We presume it is scarcely necessary to remind the reader that he is never, under any circumstances, to convey his knife to his mouth. Peas are eaten with the fork; tarts, curry, and puddings of all kinds with the spoon.

Always help fish with a fish-slice, and tart and puddings with a spoon, or, if necessary, a spoon and fork.

Asparagus must be helped with the asparagus-tongs.

In eating asparagus, it is well to observe what others do, and act accordingly. Some very well-bred people eat it with the fingers; others cut off the heads, and convey them to the mouth upon the fork. It would be difficult to say which is the more correct.

In eating stone fruit, such as cherries, damsons, &c., the same rule had better be observed. Some put the stones out from the mouth into a spoon, and so convey them to the plate. Others cover the lips with the hand, drop them unseen into the palm, and so deposit them on the side of the plate. In our own opinion, the last is the better way, as it effectually conceals the return of the stones, which is certainly the point of highest importance. Of one thing we may be sure, and that is, that they must never be dropped from the mouth to the plate.

In helping sauce, always pour it on the side of the plate.

If the servants do not go round with the wine (which is by far the best custom), the gentlemen at a dinner table should take upon themselves the office of helping those ladies who sit near them. Ladies take more wine in the present day than they did fifty years ago, and gentlemen should remember this, and offer it frequently. Ladies cannot very well ask for wine, but they can always decline it. At all events, they do not like to be neglected, or to see gentlemen liberally helping themselves, without observing whether their fair neighbours' glasses are full or empty. Young ladies seldom drink more than three glasses of wine at dinner; but married ladies, professional ladies, and those accustomed to society, and habits of affluence, will habitually take five or even six, whether in their own homes or at the tables of their friends.

The habit of taking wine with each other has almost wholly gone out of fashion. A gentleman may ask the lady whom he conducted down to dinner; or he may ask the lady of the house to take wine with him. But even these last remnants of the old custom are fast falling into disuse.

Unless you are a total abstainer, it is extremely uncivil to decline taking wine if you are invited to do so. In accepting, you have only to pour a little fresh wine into your glass, look at the person who invited you, bow slightly, and take a sip from the glass.

It is particularly ill-bred to empty your glass on these occasions.

Certain wines are taken with certain dishes, by old-established custom – as sherry, or sauterne, with soup and fish; hock and claret with roast meat; punch with turtle; champagne with whitebait; port with venison; port, or burgundy, with game; sparkling wines between the roast and the confectionery; madeira with sweets; port with cheese; and for dessert, port, tokay, madeira, sherry, and claret. Red wines should never be iced, even in summer. Claret and burgundy should always be slightly warmed; claret-cup and champagne-cup should, of course, be iced.

Instead of cooling their wines in the ice-pail, some hosts have of late years introduced clear ice upon the table, broken up in small lumps, to be put inside the glasses. This is an innovation that cannot be too strictly reprehended or too soon abolished. Melting ice can but weaken the quality and flavour of the wine. Those who desire to drink wine and water can ask for iced water if they choose, but it savours too much of economy on the part of a host to insinuate the ice inside the glasses of his guests, when the wine could be more effectually iced outside the bottle.

A silver knife and fork should be placed to each guest at dessert.

If you are asked to prepare fruit for a lady, be careful to do so, by means of the silver knife and fork only, and never to touch it with your fingers.

It is wise never to partake of any dish without knowing of what ingredients it is composed. You can always ask the servant who hands it to you, and you thereby avoid all danger of having to commit the impoliteness of leaving it, and showing that you do not approve of it.

Never speak while you have anything in your mouth.

Be careful never to taste soups or puddings till you are sure they are sufficiently cool; as, by disregarding this caution, you may be compelled to swallow what is dangerously hot, or be driven to the unpardonable alternative of returning it to your plate.

When eating or drinking, avoid every kind of audible testimony to the fact.

Finger-glasses, containing water slightly warmed and perfumed, are placed to each person at dessert. In these you may dip the tips of your fingers, wiping them afterwards on your table-napkin. If the finger-glass and doyley are placed on your dessert-plate, you should immediately remove the doyley to the left of your plate, and place the finger-glass upon it. By these means you leave the right for the wine-glasses.

Be careful to know the shapes of the various kinds of wine-glasses commonly in use, in order that you may never put forward one for another. High and narrow, and very broad and shallow glasses, are used for champagne; large, goblet-shaped glasses for burgundy and claret; ordinary wine-glasses for sherry and madeira; green glasses for hock; and somewhat large, bell-shaped glasses, for port.

Port, sherry, and madeira, are decanted. Hocks and champagnes appear in their native bottles. Claret and burgundy are handed round in a claret-jug.

Coffee and liqueurs should be handed round when the dessert has been about a quarter of an hour on the table. After this, the ladies generally retire.

Should no servant be present to do so, the gentleman who is nearest the door should hold it for the ladies to pass through.

When the ladies leave the dining-room, the gentlemen all rise in their places, and do not resume their seats till the last lady is gone.

The servants leave the room when the dessert is on the table.

If you should unfortunately overturn or break anything, do not apologise for it. You can show your regret in your face, but it is not well-bred to put it into words.

Should you injure a lady's dress, apologise amply, and assist her, if possible, to remove all traces of the damage.

To abstain from taking the last piece on the dish, or the last glass of wine in the decanter, only because it is the last, is highly ill-bred. It implies a fear that the vacancy cannot be supplied, and almost conveys an affront to your host.

In summing up the little duties and laws of the table, a popular author has said that – 'The chief matter of consideration at the dinner table – as, indeed, everywhere else in the life of a gentleman – is to be perfectly composed and at his ease. He speaks deliberately; he performs the most important act of the day as if he were performing the most ordinary. Yet there is no appearance of trifling or want of gravity in his manner; he maintains the dignity which is so becoming on so vital an occasion. He performs all the ceremonies, yet in the style of one who performs no ceremonies at all. He goes through all the complicated duties of the scene as if he were "to the manner born."'

To the giver of a dinner we have but one or two remarks to offer. If he be a bachelor, he had better give his dinner at a good hotel, or have it sent in from Birch's or Kühn's. If a married man, he will, we presume, enter into council with his wife and his cook. In any case, however, he should always bear in mind that it is his duty to entertain his friends in the best manner that his means permit; and that this is the least he can do to recompense them for the expenditure of time and money which they incur in accepting his invitation.

'To invite a friend to dinner,' says Brillat Savarin, 'is to become responsible for his happiness so long as he is under your roof.' Again: 'He who receives friends at his table, without having bestowed his personal supervision upon the repast placed before them, is unworthy to have friends.'

A dinner, to be excellent, need not consist of a great variety of dishes; but everything should be of the best, and the cookery should be perfect. That which should be cool should be cool as ice; that which should be hot should be smoking; the attendance should be rapid and noiseless; the guests well assorted; the wines of the best quality; the host attentive and courteous; the room well lighted; and the time punctual.

Every dinner should begin with soup, be followed by fish, and include some kind of game. 'The soup is to the dinner,' we are told by Grisnod de la Regnière, 'what the portico is to a building, or the overture to an opera.'

To this aphorism we may be permitted to add that a chasse of cognac or curaçoa at the close of the dinner is like the epilogue at the end of a comedy.

One more quotation and we have done:

> To perform faultlessly the honours of the table is one of the most difficult things in society. It might indeed be asserted without much fear of contradiction, that no man has as yet ever reached exact propriety in his office as host, or has hit the mean between exerting himself too much and too little. His great business is to put every one entirely at his ease, to gratify all his desires, and make him, in a word, absolutely contented with men and things. To accomplish this, he must have the genius of tact to perceive, and the genius of finesse to execute; ease and frankness of manner; a knowledge of the world that nothing can surprise; a calmness of temper that nothing can disturb; and a kindness of disposition that can never be exhausted. When he receives others he must be content to forget himself; he must relinquish all desire to shine, and even all attempts to please his guests by conversation, and rather do all in his power to let them please one another. He behaves to them without agitation, without affectation; he pays attention without an air of protection; he encourages the timid, draws out the silent, and directs conversation without sustaining it himself. He who does not do all this is wanting in his duty as host – he who does, is more than mortal.

In conclusion, we may observe that to sit long in the dining-room after the ladies have retired is to pay a bad compliment to the hostess and her fair visitors; and that it is a still worse tribute to rejoin them with a flushed face and impaired powers of thought. A refined gentleman is always temperate.

XI

THE BALL-ROOM

Invitations to a ball are issued at least ten days in advance; and this term is sometimes, in the height of the season, extended to three weeks, or even a month.

An invitation should be accepted or declined within a day or two of its reception.

Gentlemen who do not dance should not accept invitations of this kind. They are but incumbrances in the ball-room, besides which, it looks like a breach of etiquette and courtesy to stand or sit idly by when there are, most probably, ladies in the room who are waiting for an invitation to dance.

A ball generally begins about half-past nine or ten o'clock.

A man who stands up to dance without being acquainted with the figures, makes himself ridiculous, and places his partner in an embarrassing and unenviable position. There is no need for him to know the steps. It is enough if he knows how to walk gracefully through the dance, and to conduct his partner through it like a gentleman. No man can waltz too well; but to perform steps in a quadrille is not only unnecessary but *outré*.

A gentleman cannot ask a lady to dance without being first introduced to her by some member of the hostess's family.

Never enter a ball-room in other than full evening dress, and white or light kid gloves.

A gentleman cannot be too careful not to injure a lady's dress. The young men of the present day are inconceivably thoughtless in this respect, and often seem to think the mischief which they do scarcely worth an apology. Cavalry officers should never wear spurs in a ball-room.

Bear in mind that all Casino habits are to be scrupulously avoided in a private ball-room. It is an affront to a highly-bred lady to hold her hand behind you, or on your hip, when dancing a round dance. We have seen even aristocratic young men of the 'fast' genus commit these unpardonable offences against taste and decorum.

Never forget a ball-room engagement. It is the greatest neglect and slight that a gentleman can offer to a lady.

At the beginning and end of a quadrille the gentleman bows to his partner, and bows again on handing her to a seat.

After dancing, the gentleman may offer to conduct the lady to the refreshment-room.

Should a lady decline your hand for a dance, and afterwards stand up with another partner, you will do well to attribute her error to either forgetfulness or ignorance of the laws of etiquette. Politeness towards your host and hostess demands that you should never make any little personal grievance the ground of discomfort or disagreement.

A gentleman conducts his last partner to supper; waits upon her till she has had as much refreshment as she desires, and then re-conducts her to the ball-room.

However much pleasure you may take in the society of any particular lady, etiquette forbids that you should dance with her too frequently. Engaged persons would do well to bear this maxim in mind.

It is customary to call upon your entertainers within a few days after the ball.[A]

[Footnote A: For a more detailed account of the laws and business of the ball, see the chapters entitled 'The Ball-room Guide.']

XII

STAYING AT A FRIEND'S HOUSE: BREAKFAST, LUNCHEON, &c

A visitor is bound by the laws of social intercourse to conform in all respects to the habits of the house. In order to do this effectually, he should inquire, or cause his personal servant to inquire, what those habits are. To keep your friend's breakfast on the table till a late hour; to delay the dinner by want of punctuality; to accept other invitations, and treat his house as if it were merely an hotel to be slept in; or to keep the family up till unwonted hours, are alike evidences of a want of good feeling and good breeding.

At breakfast and lunch absolute punctuality is not imperative; but a visitor should avoid being always the last to appear at table.

No order of precedence is observed at either breakfast or luncheon. Persons take their seats as they come in, and, having exchanged their morning salutations, begin to eat without waiting for the rest of the party.

If letters are delivered to you at breakfast or luncheon, you may read them by asking permission from the lady who presides at the urn.

Always hold yourself at the disposal of those in whose house you are visiting. If they propose to ride, drive, walk, or otherwise occupy the day, you may take it for granted that these plans are made with reference to your enjoyment. You should, therefore, receive them with cheerfulness, enter into them with alacrity, and do your best to seem pleased, and be pleased, by the efforts which your friends make to entertain you.

You should never take a book from the library to your own room without requesting permission to borrow it. When it is lent, you should take every care that it sustains no injury while in your possession, and should cover it, if necessary.

A guest should endeavour to amuse himself as much as possible, and not be continually dependent on his hosts for entertainment. He should remember that, however welcome he may be, he is not always wanted. During the morning hours a gentleman visitor who neither shoots, reads, writes letters, nor does anything but idle about the house and chat with the ladies, is an intolerable nuisance. Sooner than become the latter, he had better retire to the billiard-room and practise cannons by himself, or pretend an engagement and walk about the neighbourhood.

Those who receive 'staying visitors,' as they are called, should remember that the truest hospitality is that which places the visitor most at his ease, and affords him the greatest opportunity for enjoyment. They should also remember that different persons have different ideas on the subject of enjoyment, and that the surest way of making a guest happy is to find out what gives him pleasure; not to impose that upon him which is pleasure to themselves.

A visitor should avoid giving unnecessary trouble to the servants of the house, and should be liberal to them when he leaves.

The signal for retiring to rest is generally given by the appearance of the servant with wine, water, and biscuits, where a late dinner-hour is observed and suppers are not the custom. This is the last refreshment of the evening, and the visitor will do well to rise and wish good-night shortly after it has been partaken of by the family.

GENERAL HINTS

In entering a morning exhibition, or public room, where ladies are present, the gentleman should lift his hat.

In going upstairs the gentleman should precede the lady; in goingdown, he should follow her.

If you accompany ladies to a theatre or concert-room, precede them to clear the way and secure their seats.

Do not frequently repeat the name of the person with whom you are conversing. It implies either the extreme of hauteur or familiarity. We have already cautioned you against the repetition of titles. Deference can always be better expressed in the voice, manner, and countenance than in any forms of words.

If when you are walking with a lady in any crowded thoroughfare you are obliged to proceed singly, always precede her.

Always give the lady the wall; by doing so you interpose your own person between her and the passers by, and assign her the cleanest part of the pavement.

At public balls, theatres, &c., a gentleman should never permit the lady to pay for refreshments, vehicles, and so forth. If she insists on repaying him afterwards, he must of course defer to her wishes.

Never speak of absent persons by only their Christian or surnames; but always as Mr. — or Mrs. —. Above all, never name anybody by the first letter of his name. Married people are sometimes guilty of this flagrant offence against taste.

If you are smoking and meet a lady to whom you wish to speak, immediately throw away your cigar.

Do not smoke shortly before entering the presence of ladies.

A young man who visits frequently at the house of a married friend may be permitted to show his sense of the kindness which he receives by the gift of a Christmas or New Year's volume to the wife or daughter of his entertainer. The presentation of *Etrennes* is now carried to a ruinous and ludicrous height among our French neighbours; but it should be remembered that, without either ostentation or folly, a gift ought to be worth offering. It is better to give nothing than too little. On the other hand, mere costliness does not constitute the soul of a present; on the contrary, it has the commercial and unflattering effect of repayment for value received.

A gift should be precious for something better than its price. It may have been brought by the giver from some far or famous place; it may be unique in its workmanship; it may be valuable only from association with some great man or strange event. Autographic papers, foreign curiosities, and the like, are elegant gifts. An author may offer his book, or a painter a sketch, with grace and propriety. Offerings of flowers and game are unexceptionable, and may be made even to those whose position is superior to that of the giver.

If you present a book to a friend, do not write his or her name in it, unless requested. You have no right to presume that it will be rendered any the more valuable for that addition; and you ought not to conclude beforehand that your gift will be accepted.

Never refuse a present unless under very exceptional circumstances. However humble the giver, and however poor the gift, you should appreciate the goodwill and intention, and accept it with kindness and thanks. Never say 'I fear I rob you,' or 'I am really ashamed to take it,' &c., &c. Such deprecatory phrases imply that you think the bestower of the gift cannot spare or afford it.

Never undervalue the gift which you are yourself offering; you have no business to offer it if it is valueless. Neither say that you do not want it yourself, or that you should throw it away if it were not accepted. Such apologies would be insults if true, and mean nothing if false.

No compliment that bears insincerity on the face of it is a compliment at all.

To yawn in the presence of others, to lounge, to put your feet on a chair, to stand with your back to the fire, to take the most comfortable seat in the room, to do anything which shows indifference, selfishness, or disrespect, is unequivocally vulgar and inadmissible.

If a person of greater age or higher rank than yourself desires you to step first into a carriage, or through a door, it is more polite to bow and obey than to decline.

Compliance with, and deference to, the wishes of others is the finest breeding.

When you cannot agree with the propositions advanced in general conversation, be silent. If pressed for your opinion, give it with modesty. Never defend your own views too warmly. When you find others remain unconvinced, drop the subject, or lead to some other topic.

Look at those who address you.

Never boast of your birth, your money, your grand friends, or anything that is yours. If you have travelled, do not introduce that information into your conversation at every opportunity. Anyone can travel with money and leisure. The real distinction is to come home with enlarged views, improved tastes, and a mind free from prejudice.

Give a foreigner his name in full, as Monsieur de Vigny – never as Monsieur only. In speaking of him, give him his title, if he has one. Foreign noblemen are addressed viva voce as Monsieur. In speaking of a foreign nobleman before his face, say Monsieur le Comte, or Monsieur le Marquis. In his absence, say Monsieur le Comte de Vigny.

Converse with a foreigner in his own language. If not competent to do so, apologise, and beg permission to speak English.

Etiquette of Courtship
and Matrimony

I

FIRST STEPS IN
COURTSHIP

It would be out of place in these pages to grapple with a subject so large
as that of Love in its varied phases: a theme that must be left to poets,
novelists, and moralists to dilate upon. It is sufficient for our purpose to
recognise the existence of this the most universal – the most powerful
– of human passions, when venturing to offer our counsel and guidance
to those of both sexes who, under its promptings, have resolved to become
votaries of Hymen, but who, from imperfect knowledge of conventional
usages, are naturally apprehensive that at every step they take, they may
render themselves liable to misconception, ridicule, or censure.

We will take it for granted, then, that a gentleman has in one way or
another become fascinated by a fair lady – possibly a recent acquaint-
ance--whom he is most anxious to know more particularly. His heart
already feels 'the inly touch of love,' and his most ardent wish is to have
that love returned.

At this point we venture to give him a word of serious advice. We
urge him, before he ventures to take any step towards the pursuit of
this object, to consider well his position and prospects in life, and reflect
whether they are such as to justify him in deliberately seeking to win the
young lady's affections, with the view of making her his wife at no distant
period. Should he after such a review of his affairs feel satisfied that he
can proceed honourably, he may then use fair opportunities to ascertain
the estimation in which the young lady, as well as her family, is held by
friends. It is perhaps needless to add, that all possible delicacy and caution
must be observed in making such inquiries, so as to avoid compromising the lady herself in the slightest degree. When he has satisfied himself

on this head, and found no insurmountable impediment in his way, his next endeavour will be, through the mediation of a common friend, to procure an introduction to the lady's family. Those who undertake such an office incur no slight responsibility, and are, of course, expected to be scrupulously careful in performing it, and to communicate all they happen to know affecting the character and circumstances of the individual they introduce.

We will now reverse the picture, and see how matters stand on the fair one's side.

First let us hope that the inclination is mutual; at all events, that the lady views her admirer with preference, that she deems him not unworthy of her favourable regard, and that his attentions are agreeable to her. It is true her heart may not yet be won: she has to be wooed; and what fair daughter of Eve has not hailed with rapture that brightest day in the springtide of her life? She has probably first met the gentleman at a ball, or other festive occasion, where the excitement of the scene has reflected on every object around a roseate tint. We are to suppose, of course, that in looks, manner, and address, her incipient admirer is not below her ideal standard in gentlemanly attributes. His respectful approaches to her – in soliciting her hand as a partner in the dance, &c. – have first awakened on her part a slight feeling of interest towards him. This mutual feeling of interest, once established, soon 'grows by what it feeds on.' The exaltation of the whole scene favours its development, and it can hardly be wondered at if both parties leave judgment 'out in the cold' while enjoying each other's society, and possibly already pleasantly occupied in building 'castles in the air.' Whatever may eventually come of it, the fair one is conscious for the nonce of being unusually happy. This emotion is not likely to be diminished when she finds herself the object of general attention – accompanied, it may be, by the display of a little envy among rival beauties – owing to the assiduous homage of her admirer. At length, prudence whispers that he is to her, as yet, but a comparative stranger; and with a modest reserve she endeavours to retire from his observation, so as not to seem to encourage his attentions. The gentleman's ardour, however, is not to be thus checked; he again solicits her to be his partner in a dance. She finds it hard, very hard, to refuse him; and both, yielding at last to the alluring influences by which they are surrounded, discover at the moment of parting that a new and delightful sensation has been awakened in their hearts.

At a juncture so critical in the life of a young inexperienced woman as that when she begins to form an attachment for one of the opposite sex – at a moment when she needs the very best advice accompanied with a considerate regard for her overwrought feelings – the very best course she can take is to confide the secret of her heart to that truest and most loving of friends – her mother. Fortunate is the daughter who has not been deprived of that wisest and tenderest of counsellors–whose experience of life, whose prudence and sagacity, whose anxious care and appreciation of her child's sentiments, and whose awakened recollections of her own trysting days, qualify and entitle her above all other beings to counsel and comfort her trusting child, and to claim her confidence. Let the timid girl then pour forth into her mother's ear the flood of her pent-up feelings. Let her endeavour to distrust her own judgment, and seek hope, guidance, and support from one who, she well knows, will not deceive or mislead her. The confidence thus established will be productive of the most beneficial results – by securing the daughter's obedience to her parent's advice, and her willing adoption of the observances prescribed by etiquette, which, as the courtship progresses, that parent will not fail to recommend as strictly essential in this phase of life. Where a young woman has had the misfortune to be deprived of her mother, she should at such a period endeavour to find her next best counsellor in some female relative, or other trustworthy friend.

We are to suppose that favourable opportunities for meeting have occurred, until, by-and-by, both the lady and her admirer have come to regard each other with such warm feelings of inclination as to have a constant craving for each other's society. Other eyes have in the meantime not failed to notice the symptoms of a growing attachment; and some 'kind friends' have, no doubt, even set them down as already engaged.

The admirer of the fair one is, indeed, so much enamoured as to be unable longer to retain his secret within his own breast; and, not being without hope that his attachment is reciprocated, resolves on seeking an introduction to the lady's family preparatory to his making a formal declaration of love.

It is possible, however, that the lover's endeavours to procure the desired introduction may fail of success, although, where no material difference of social position exists, this difficulty will be found to occur less frequently than might at first be supposed. He must then discreetly adopt measures to bring himself in some degree under the fair one's notice: such, for instance, as attending the place of worship which she frequents, meeting her, so often as to be manifestly for the purpose, in the course of her promenades, &c. He will thus soon be able to judge – even without speaking to the lady – whether his further attentions will be distasteful to her. The signs of this on the lady's part, though of the most trifling nature, and in no way compromising her, will be unmistakeable; for, as the poet tells us in speaking of the sex:

He gave them but one tongue to say us 'Nay,'
And two fond eyes to grant!

Should her demeanour be decidedly discouraging, any perseverance on his part would be ungentlemanly and highly indecorous. But, on the other hand, should a timid blush intimate doubt, or a gentle smile lurking in the half-dropped eye give pleasing challenge to further parley when possible, he may venture to write – not to the lady—that would be the opening of a clandestine correspondence, an unworthy course where every act should be open and straightforward, as tending to manly and honourable ends – but, to the father or guardian, through the agency of a common friend where feasible; or, in some instances, to the party at whose residence the lady may be staying. In his letter he ought first to state his position in life and prospects, as well as mention his family connections; and then to request permission to visit the family, as a preliminary step to paying his addresses to the object of his admiration.

By this course he in no wise compromises either himself or the lady; but leaves open to both, at any future period, an opportunity of retiring from the position of courtship taken up on the one side, and of receiving addresses on the other, without laying either party open to the accusation of fickleness or jilting.

II

ETIQUETTE OF COURTSHIP

In whatever way the attachment may have originated, whether resulting from old association or from a recent acquaintanceship between the lovers, we will assume that the courtship is so far in a favourable train that the lady's admirer has succeeded in obtaining an introduction to her family, and that he is about to be received in their domestic circle on the footing of a welcome visitor, if not yet in the light of a probationary suitor.

In the first case, matters will in all probability be found to amble on so calmly, that the enamoured pair may seldom find it needful to consult the rules of etiquette; but in the latter, its rules must be attentively observed, or 'the course of true love' will assuredly not run smooth.

If the gentleman be a person of good breeding and right feeling, he will need no caution from us to remember that, when he is admitted into the heart of a family as the suitor of a daughter, he is receiving one of the greatest possible favours that can be conferred on him, whatever may be his own superiority of social rank or worldly circumstances; and that, therefore, his conduct should be marked by a delicate respect towards the parents of his lady-love. By this means he will propitiate them in his favour, and induce them to regard him as worthy of the trust they have placed in him.

Young people are naturally prone to seek the company of those they love; and as their impulses are often at such times impatient of control, etiquette prescribes cautionary rules for the purpose of averting the mischief that unchecked intercourse and incautious familiarity might give rise to. For instance, a couple known to be attached to each other should never, unless when old acquaintances, be left alone for any length of time, nor be allowed to meet in any other place than the lady's home – particularly at balls, concerts, and other public places – except in the presence of a third party. This, as a general rule, should be carefully observed, although exceptions may occasionally occur under special circumstances; but even then the full consent of the lady's nearest relatives or guardians should be previously obtained.

What the Lady should observe during Courtship

A lady should be particular during the early days of courtship – while still retaining some clearness of mental vision – to observe the manner in which her suitor comports himself to other ladies. If he behaves with ease and courtesy, without freedom or the slightest approach to licence in manner or conversation; if he never speaks slightingly of the sex, and be ever ready to honour its virtues and defend its weakness; she may continue to incline towards him a willing ear. His habits and his conduct must awaken her vigilant attention before it be too late. Should he come to visit her at irregular hours; should he exhibit a vague or wandering attention – give proofs of a want of punctuality – show disrespect for age – sneer at things sacred, or absent himself from regular attendance at divine service – or evince an inclination to expensive pleasures beyond his means, or to low and vulgar amusements; should he be foppish, eccentric, or very slovenly in his dress; or display a frivolity of mind, and an absence of well-directed energy in his worldly pursuits; let the young lady, we say, while there is yet time, eschew that gentleman's acquaintance, and allow it gently to drop. The effort, at whatever cost to her feelings, must be made, if she have any regard for her future happiness and self-respect. The proper course then to take is to intimate her distaste, and the causes that have given rise to it, to her parents or guardian, who will be pretty sure to sympathise with her, and to take measures for facilitating the retirement of the gentleman from his pretensions.

What the Gentleman should observe during Courtship

It would be well also for the suitor, on his part, during the first few weeks of courtship, carefully to observe the conduct of the young lady in her own family, and the degree of estimation in which she is held by them, as well as amongst her intimate friends. If she be attentive to her duties; respectful and affectionate to her parents; kind and forbearing to her brothers and sisters; not easily ruffled in temper; if her mind be prone to cheerfulness and to hopeful aspiration, instead of to the display of a morbid anxiety and dread of coming evil; if her pleasures and enjoyments be those which chiefly centre in home; if her words be characterised by benevolence, goodwill, and charity: then we say, let him not hesitate, but hasten to enshrine so precious a gem in the casket of his affections. But if, on the other hand, he should find that he has been attracted by the tricksome affectation and heartless allurements of a flirt, ready to bestow smiles on all, but with a heart for none; if she who has succeeded for a time in fascinating him be of uneven temper, easily provoked, and slow to be appeased; fond of showy dress, and eager for admiration; ecstatic about trifles, frivolous in her tastes, and weak and wavering in performing her duties; if her religious observances are merely the formality of lip service; if she be petulant to her friends, pert and disrespectful to her parents, overbearing to her inferiors; if pride, vanity, and affectation be her characteristics; if she be inconstant in her friendships; gaudy and slovenly, rather than neat and scrupulously clean, in attire and personal habits: then we counsel the gentleman to retire as speedily but as politely as possible from the pursuit of an object quite unworthy of his admiration and love; nor dread that the lady's friends – who must know her better than he can do – will call him to account for withdrawing from the field.

But we will take it for granted that all goes on well; that the parties are, on sufficient acquaintance, pleased with each other, and that the gentleman is eager to prove the sincerity of his affectionate regard by giving some substantial token of his love and homage to the fair one. This brings us to the question of ...

Presents

... a point on which certain observances of etiquette must not be disregarded. A lady, for instance, cannot with propriety accept presents from a gentleman previously to his having made proposals of marriage. She would by so doing incur an obligation at once embarrassing and unbecoming. Should, however, the gentleman insist on making her a present – as of some trifling article of jewellery, &c., – there must be no secret about it. Let the young lady take an early opportunity of saying to her admirer, in the presence of her father or mother, 'I am much obliged to you for that ring [or other trinket, as the case may be] which you kindly offered me the other day, and which I shall be most happy to accept, if my parents do not object;' and let her say this in a manner which, while it increases the obligation, will divest it altogether of impropriety, from having been conferred under the sanction of her parents.

We have now reached that stage, in the progress of the courtship where budding affection, having developed into mature growth, encourages the lover to make ...

The Proposal

When about to take this step, the suitor's first difficulty is how to get a favourable opportunity; and next, having got the chance, how to screw his courage up to give utterance to the 'declaration.' We have heard of a young lover who carried on a courtship for four months ere he could obtain a private interview with his lady-love. In the house, as might be expected, they were never left alone; and in a walk a third party always accompanied them. In such a dilemma, ought he to have unburdened his heart of its secret through the medium of a letter? We say not. A declaration in writing should certainly be avoided where the lover can by any possibility get at the lady's ear. But there are cases where this is so difficult that an impatient lover cannot be restrained from adopting the agency of a *billet-doux* in declaring his passion.

The lady, before proposal, is generally prepared for it. It is seldom that such an avowal comes without some previous indications of look and manner on the part of the admirer, which can hardly fail of being understood. She may not, indeed, consider herself engaged; and, although nearly certain of the conquest she has made, may yet have her misgivings. Some gentlemen dread to ask, lest they should be refused. Many pause just at the point, and refrain from anything like ardour in their professions of attachment until they feel confident that they may be spared the mortification and ridicule that is supposed to attach to being rejected, in addition to the pain of disappointed hope. This hesitation when the mind is made up is wrong; but it does often occur, and we suppose ever will do so, with persons of great timidity of character. By it both parties are kept needlessly on the fret, until the long-looked-for opportunity unexpectedly arrives, when the flood-gates of feeling are loosened, and the full tide of mutual affection gushes forth uncontrolled. It is, however, at this moment – the agony-point to the embarrassed lover, who 'doats yet doubts' – whose suppressed feelings render him morbidly sensitive

– that a lady should be especially careful lest any show of either prudery or coquetry on her part should lose to her for ever the object of her choice. True love is generally delicate and timid, and may easily be scared by affected indifference, through feelings of wounded pride. A lover needs very little to assure him of the reciprocation of his attachment: a glance, a single pressure of hand, a whispered syllable on the part of the loved one, will suffice to confirm his hopes.

Refusal by the Young Lady

When a lady rejects the proposal of a gentleman, her behaviour should be characterised by the most delicate feeling towards one who, in offering her his hand, has proved his desire to confer upon her, by this implied preference for her above all other women, the greatest honour it is in his power to offer. Therefore, if she have no love for him, she ought at least to evince a tender regard for his feelings; and, in the event of her being previously engaged, should at once acquaint him with the fact. No right-minded man would desire to persist in a suit when he well knew that the object of his admiration has already disposed of her heart.

When a gentleman makes an offer of his hand by letter, the letter must be answered, and certainly not returned, should the answer be a refusal; unless, indeed, when, from a previous repulse, or some other particular and special circumstances, such an offer may be regarded by the lady or her relatives as presumptuous and intrusive. Under such circumstances, the letter may be placed by the lady in the hands of her parents or guardian, to be dealt with by them as they may deem most advisable.

No woman of proper feeling would regard her rejection of an offer of marriage from a worthy man as a matter of triumph: her feeling on such an occasion should be one of regretful sympathy with him for the pain she is unavoidably compelled to inflict. Nor should such a rejection be unaccompanied with some degree of self examination on her part, to discern whether any lightness of demeanour or tendency to flirtation may have given rise to a false hope of her favouring his suit. At all events, no lady should ever treat the man who has so honoured her with the slightest disrespect or frivolous disregard, nor ever unfeelingly parade a more favoured suitor before one whom she has refused.

Conduct of the Gentleman when his Addresses are rejected

The conduct of the gentleman under such distressing circumstances should be characterised by extreme delicacy and a chivalrous resolve to avoid occasioning any possible annoyance or uneasiness to the fair author of his pain. If, however, he should have reason to suppose that his rejection has resulted from mere indifference to his suit, he need not altogether retire from the field, but may endeavour to kindle a feeling of regard and sympathy for the patient endurance of his disappointment, and for his continued but respectful endeavours to please the lukewarm fair one. But in the case of avowed or evident preference for another, it becomes imperative upon him, as a gentleman, to withdraw at once, and so relieve the lady of any obstacle that his presence or pretensions may occasion to the furtherance of her obvious wishes. A pertinacious continuance of his attentions, on the part of one who has been distinctly rejected, is an insult deserving of the severest reprobation. Although the weakness of her sex, which ought to be her protection, frequently prevents a woman from forcibly breaking off an acquaintance thus annoyingly forced upon her, she rarely fails to resent such impertinence by that sharpest of woman's weapons, a keen-edged but courteous ridicule, which few men can bear up against.

Refusal by the Lady's Parents or Guardians

It may happen that both the lady and her suitor are willing; but that the parents or guardians of the former, on being referred to, deem the connection unfitting, and refuse their consent. In this state of matters, the first thing a man of sense, proper feeling, and candour should do, is to endeavour to learn the objections of the parents, to see whether they cannot be removed. If they are based on his present insufficiency of means, a lover of a persevering spirit may effect much in removing apprehension on that score, by cheerfully submitting to a reasonable time of probation, in the hope of amelioration in his worldly circumstances. Happiness delayed will be none the less precious when love has stood the test of constancy and the trial of time. Should the objection be founded on inequality of social position, the parties, if young, may wait until matured age shall ripen their judgment and place the future more at their own disposal. A clandestine marriage should be peremptorily declined. In too many cases it is a fraud committed by an elder and more experienced party upon one whose ignorance of the world's ways and whose confiding tenderness appeal to him for protection even against himself. In nearly all the instances we have known of such marriages, the results proved the step to have been ill-judged, imprudent, and highly injurious to the reputation of one party, and in the long run detrimental to the happiness of both.

III

ETIQUETTE OF AN ENGAGEMENT

We will now regard the pair of lovers as formally engaged, and bound together in that state of approximation to marriage which was in the ancient Christian Church, and indeed is still in many countries of Europe, considered in a very sacred light, little inferior to, and, in fact, regarded as a part of, marriage itself – the Betrothment.

Conduct of the Engaged Couple

The conduct of the bridegroom-elect should be marked by a gallant and affectionate assiduity towards his lady-love – a *dévouement* easily felt and understood, but not so easy to define. That of the lady towards him should manifest delicacy, tenderness, and confidence; while looking for his thorough devotion to herself, she should not captiously take offence and show airs at his showing the same kind of attention to other ladies as she, in her turn, would not hesitate to receive from the other sex.

In the behaviour of a gentleman towards his betrothed in public, little difference should be perceptible from his demeanour to other ladies, except in those minute attentions which none but those who love can properly understand or appreciate.

In private, the slightest approach to indecorous familiarity must be avoided; indeed, it is pretty certain to be resented by every woman who deserves to be a bride. The lady's honour is now in her lover's hands, and he should never forget in his demeanour to and before her that that lady is to be his future wife.

It is the privilege of the betrothed lover, as it is also his duty, to give advice to the fair one who now implicitly confides in him. Should he detect a fault, should he observe failings which he would wish removed or amended, let him avail himself of this season, so favourable for the frank interchange of thought between the betrothed pair, to urge their correction. He will find a ready listener; and any judicious counsel offered to her by him will now be gratefully received and remembered in after life. After marriage it may be too late; for advice on trivial points of conduct may then not improbably be resented by the wife as an unnecessary interference: now, the fair and loving creature is disposed like pliant wax in his hands to mould herself to his reasonable wishes in all things.

Conduct of the Lady during her Betrothal

A lady is not expected to keep aloof from society on her engagement, nor to debar herself from the customary attentions and courtesies of her male acquaintances generally; but she should, while accepting them cheerfully, maintain such a prudent reserve, as to intimate that they are viewed by her as mere acts of ordinary courtesy and friendship. In all places of public amusement – at balls, the opera, &c – for a lady to be seen with any other cavalier than her avowed lover in close attendance upon her would expose her to the imputation of flirtation. She will naturally take pains at such a period to observe the taste of her lover in regard to her costume, and strive carefully to follow it, for all men desire to have their taste and wishes on such apparent trifles gratified. She should at the same time observe much delicacy in regard to dress, and be careful to avoid any unseemly display of her charms: lovers are naturally jealous of observation under such circumstances. It is a mistake not seldom made by women, to suppose their suitors will be pleased by the glowing admiration expressed by other men for the object of their passion. Most lovers, on the contrary, we believe, would prefer to withdraw their prize from general observation until the happy moment for their union has arrived.

Conduct of the Gentleman towards the Family of his Betrothed

The lover, having now secured his position, should use discretion and tact in his intercourse with the lady's family, and take care that his visits be not deemed too frequent so as to be really inconvenient to them. He should accommodate himself as much as possible to their habits and ways, and be ever ready and attentive to consult their wishes. Marked attention, and in most cases affectionate kindness, to the lady's mother ought to be shown: such respectful homage will secure for him many advantages in his present position. He must not, however, presume to take his stand yet as a member of the family, nor exhibit an obtrusive familiarity in manner and conversation. Should a disruption of the engagement from some unexpected cause ensue, it is obvious that any such premature assumption would lead to very embarrassing results. In short, his conduct should be such as to win for himself the esteem and affection of all the family, and dispose them ever to welcome and desire his presence, rather than regard him as an intruder.

Conduct of the Lady on Retiring from her Engagement

Should this step unhappily be found necessary on the lady's part, the truth should be spoken, and the reasons frankly given: there must be no room left for the suspicion of its having originated in caprice or injustice. The case should be so put that the gentleman himself must see and acknowledge the justice of the painful decision arrived at. Incompatible habits, ungentlemanly actions, anything tending to diminish that respect for the lover which should be felt for the husband; inconstancy, ill-governed temper – all which, not to mention other obvious objections – are to be considered as sufficient reasons for terminating an engagement. The communication should be made as tenderly as possible: room may be left in mere venial cases for reformation; but all that is done must be so managed that not the slightest shadow of fickleness or want of faith may rest upon the character of the lady. It must be remembered, however, that the termination of an engagement by a lady has the privilege of passing unchallenged, – a lady not being bound to declare any other reason than her will. Nevertheless she owes it to her own reputation that her decision should rest on a sufficient foundation, and be unmistakably pronounced.

Conduct of the Gentleman on Retiring from his Engagement

We hardly know how to approach this portion of our subject. The reasons must be strong indeed that can sufficiently justify a man, placed in the position of an accepted suitor, in severing the ties by which he has bound himself to a lady with the avowed intention of making her his wife. His reasons for breaking off his engagement must be such as will not merely satisfy his own conscience, but will justify him in the eyes of the world. If the fault be on the lady's side, great reserve and delicacy will be observed by any man of honour. If, on the other hand, the imperative force of circumstances, such as loss of fortune, or some other unexpected calamity to himself, may be the cause, then must the reason be clearly and fully explained, in such a manner as to soothe the painful feelings which such a result must necessarily occasion to the lady and her friends. It is scarcely necessary to point out the necessity for observing great caution in all that relates to the antecedents of an engagement that has been broken off; especially the return on either side of presents and of all letters that have passed.

This last allusion brings us to the consideration of …

Correspondence

Letter-writing is one great test of ability and cultivation, as respects both sexes. The imperfections of education may be to some extent concealed or glossed over in conversation, but cannot fail to stand out conspicuously in a letter. An ill-written letter infallibly betrays the vulgarity and ignorance indicative of a mean social position.

But there is something more to be guarded against than even bad writing and worse spelling in a correspondence: saying too much – writing that kind of matter which will not bear to be read by other eyes than those for which it was originally intended. That this is too frequently done is amply proved by the love letters often read in a court of law, the most affecting passages from which occasion 'roars of laughter' and the derisive comments of merry-making counsel. Occurrences of this kind prove how frequently letters are not returned or burnt when an affair of the heart is broken off. Correspondence between lovers should at all events be tempered with discretion; and, on the lady's part particularly, her affectionate expressions should not degenerate into a silly style of fondness.

It is as well to remark here, that in correspondence between a couple not actually engaged, the use of Christian names in addressing each other should be avoided.

Demeanour of the Suitor during Courtship

The manners of a gentleman are ever characterized by urbanity and a becoming consideration for the feelings and wishes of others, and by a readiness to practise self-denial. But the very nature of courtship requires the fullest exercise of these excellent qualities on his part. The lover should carefully accommodate his tone and bearing, whether cheerful or serious, to the mood for the time of his lady-love, whose slightest wish must be his law. In his assiduities to her he must allow of no stint; though hindered by time, distance, or fatigue, he must strive to make his professional and social duties bend to his homage at the shrine of love. All this can be done, moreover, by a man of excellent sense with perfect propriety. Indeed, the world will not only commend him for such devoted gallantry, but will be pretty sure to censure him for any short-coming in his performance of such devoirs.

It is, perhaps, needless to observe that at such a period a gentleman should be scrupulously neat, without appearing particular, in his attire. We shall not attempt to prescribe what he should wear, as that must, of course, depend on the times of the day when his visits are paid, and other circumstances, such as meeting a party of friends, going to the theatre, &c., with the lady.

Should a Courtship be Short or Long?

The answer to this question must depend on the previous acquaintance-ship, connection, or relationship of the parties, as well as on their present circumstances, and the position of their parents. In case of relation-ship or old acquaintanceship subsisting between the families, when the courtship, declaration, and engagement have followed each other rapidly, a short wooing is preferable to a long one, should other circumstances not create an obstacle. Indeed, as a general rule, we are disposed strongly to recommend a short courtship. A man is never well settled in the saddle of his fortunes until he be married. He wants spring, purpose, and aim; and, above all, he wants a home as the centre of his efforts. Some portion of inconvenience, therefore, may be risked to obtain this; in fact, it often occurs that by waiting too long the freshness of life is worn off, and that the generous glow of early feelings becomes tamed down to lukewarmness by a too prudent delaying; while a slight sacrifice of ambition or self-indulgence on the part of the gentleman, and a little descent from pride of station on the lady's side, might have ensured years of satisfied love and happy wedded life.

On the other hand, we would recommend a long courtship as advisable when – the friends on both sides favouring the match – it happens that the fortune of neither party will prudently allow an immediate marriage. The gentleman, we will suppose, has his way to make in his profession or business, and is desirous not to involve the object of his affection in the distressing inconvenience, if not the misery, of straitened means. He reflects that for a lady it is an actual degradation, however love may ennoble the motive of her submission, to descend from her former footing in society. He feels, therefore, that this risk ought not to be incurred. For, although the noble and loving spirit of a wife might enable her to bear up cheerfully against misfortune, and by her endearments soothe the broken spirit of her husband; yet the lover who would wilfully, at the outset of wedded life, expose his devoted helpmate to the ordeal of poverty, would be deservedly scouted as selfish and unworthy. These, then, are among the circumstances which warrant a lengthened engagement, and it should be the endeavour of the lady's friends to approve such cautious delay, and do all they can to assist the lover in his efforts to abridge it. The lady's father should regard the lover in the light of another son added to his family, and spare no pains to promote his interests in life, while the lady's mother should do everything in her power, by those small attentions which a mother understands so well, to make the protracted engagement agreeable to him, and as endurable as possible to her daughter.

IV

PRELIMINARY ETIQUETTE OF A WEDDING

Whether the term of courtship may have been long or short – according to the requirements of the case – the time will at last arrive for ...

Fixing the Day

While it is the gentleman's province to press for the earliest possible opportunity, it is the lady's privilege to name the happy day; not but that the bridegroom-elect must, after all, issue the fiat, for he has much to consider and prepare for beforehand: for instance, to settle where it will be most convenient to spend the honeymoon – a point which must depend on the season of the year, on his own vocation, and other circumstances. At this advanced state of affairs, we must not overlook the important question of ...

Legal Settlements

These are matters that must be attended to where there is property on either side; and it behoves the intending bridegroom to take care there is no unnecessary delay in completing them. An occasional morning call in one of the Inns of Court at this period is often found to be necessary to hasten the usually sluggish pace of the legal fraternity. On the business part of this matter it is not the province of our work to dilate; but we may be permitted to suggest that two-thirds, or at least one-half, of the lady's property should be settled on herself and offspring; and that where the bridegroom has no property wherewith to endow his wife, and has solely to rely on his professional prospects, it should be made a *sine qua non* that he should insure his life in her favour previously to marriage.

How to be Married

By this time the gentleman will have made up his mind in what form he will be married – a question, the solution of which, however, must chiefly depend on his means and position in life. He has his choice whether he will be married by banns, by licence, by special licence, or before the Registrar; but woe betide the unlucky wight who should venture to suggest the last method to a young lady or her parents!

Marriage by Banns

For this purpose, notice must be given to the clerk of the parish or of the district church. The names of the two parties must be written down in full, with their conditions, and the parishes in which they reside – as, 'Between A.B, of the parish of St. George, bachelor [or widower, as the case may be], and C.D, of the parish of St. George, spinster [or widow, as the case may be].' No mention of either the lady's or gentleman's age is required. Where the lady and gentleman are of different parishes, the banns must be published in each, and a certificate of their publication in the one furnished to the clergyman who may marry the parties in the church of the other parish.

It seems singular, albeit it is the fact, that no evidence of consent by either party is necessary to this 'putting up of the banns,' as is it denominated; indeed, the publication of the banns is not infrequently the first rural declaration of attachment, so that the blushing village maiden sometimes finds herself announced as a bride-elect before she has received any actual declaration. The clerk receives his fee of two shillings and makes no further inquiries; nay, more, is prepared, if required, to provide the necessary fathers on each side, in the respectable persons of himself and the sexton – the venerable pew-opener being also ready, on a pinch, to 'perform' the part of bridesmaid.

The banns must be publicly read on three successive Sundays in the church, after the last of which, if they so choose, the happy pair may, on the Monday following, be 'made one.' It is usual to give one day's previous notice to the clerk; but this is not legally necessary, it being the care of the Church, as well as the policy of the Law, to throw as few impediments as possible in the way of marriage, of which the one main fact of a consent to live together, declared publicly before an assemblage of relatives, friends, and neighbours (and afterwards, as it were by legal deduction, before witnesses), is the essential and constituent element. Marriage by banns, except in the country districts, is usually confined to the humbler classes of society. This is to be regretted, in as much as it is a more deliberate and solemn declaration, and leaves the ceremony more free from the imputation of suddenness, contrivance, or fraud, than any other form. A marriage by banns, it is understood, can never be set aside by the after discovery of deception or concealment as respects residence, and even names, on either side. The fees of a marriage by banns vary from 11*s*. 6*d*. to 13*s*. 6*d*. and 15*s*. 6*d*., according to the parish or district wherein the marriage may take place.

Hours in which Marriages may be Celebrated

All marriages at church must be celebrated within canonical hours – that is, between the hours of eight and twelve, except in the case of special licence, when the marriage may be celebrated at any hour, or at any 'meet and proper place.'

Marriage by Special Licence

By the Statute of 23rd Henry VIII., the Archbishop of Canterbury has power to grant special licences; but in a certain sense these are limited. His Grace restricts his authority to Peers and Peeresses in their own right, to their sons and daughters, to Dowager Peeresses, to Privy Councillors, to Judges of the Courts at Westminster, to Baronets and Knights, and to Members of Parliament; and, by an order of a former Prelate, to no other person is a special licence to be given, unless they allege very strong and weighty reasons for such indulgence, arising from particular circumstances of the case, the truth of which must be proved to the satisfaction of the Archbishop.

The application for a special licence is to be made to his Grace through the proctor of the parties, who, having first ascertained names and particulars, will wait upon his Grace for his fiat.

The expense of a special licence is about twenty-eight or thirty guineas, whereas that of an ordinary licence is but two guineas and a half; or three guineas where the gentleman or lady, or both, are minors.

Marriage by Licence

An ordinary marriage licence is to be obtained at the Faculty Registry, or Vicar-General's Office, or Diocesan Registry Office of the Archbishops or Bishops, either in the country, or at Doctors' Commons, or by applying to a proctor. A licence from Doctors' Commons, unlike others, however, is available throughout the whole of England.

The gentleman or lady (for either may attend), before applying for an ordinary marriage licence, should ascertain in what parish or district they are both residing – the church of such parish or district being the church in which the marriage should be celebrated; and either the gentleman or lady must have had his or her usual abode therein fifteen days before application is made for the licence, as the following form, to be made on oath, sets forth:

Proctor. LICENCE, Dated 187—.

'VICAR-GENERAL'S OFFICE.' 187—.

Appeared personally, A.B., of the parish or district of —, in the county of —, a bachelor, of the age of 21 years and upwards, and prayed a Licence for the solemnisation of matrimony in the parish or district church of —, between him and C.D., of the district of —, in the county of —, a spinster, of the age of 21 years or upwards, and made oath, that he believeth that there is no impediment of kindred or alliance, or of any other lawful cause, nor any suit commenced in any Ecclesiastical Court, to bar or hinder the proceeding of the said matrimony, according to the tenor of such Licence. And he further made oath, that he, the said A.B. or C.D., hath had his [or her] usual place of abode within the said parish or district of —, for the space of fifteen days last past.

Sworn before me, [Here the document must be signed by the Vicar-General, or a Surrogate appointed by him.]

This affidavit having been completed, the licence is then made out. It runs thus:

> Archibald Campbell, by Divine Providence Archbishop of Canterbury, Primate of all England, and Metropolitan, To our well beloved in Christ, A.B., of —, and C.D., of —, Grace and Health. Whereas ye are, as it is alleged, resolved to proceed to the solemnisation of true and lawful matrimony, and that you greatly desire that the same may be solemnised in the face of the Church: We, being willing that these your honest desires may the more speedily obtain a due effect, and to the end therefore that this marriage may be publicly and lawfully solemnised in the church of —, by the Rector, Vicar, or Curate thereof, without the publication or proclamation of the banns of matrimony, provided there shall appear no impediment of kindred or alliance, or of any other lawful cause, nor any suit commenced in any Ecclesiastical Court, to bar or hinder the proceeding of the said matrimony, according to the tenor of this Licence; And likewise, that the celebration of this marriage be had and done publicly in the aforesaid — church, between the hours of eight and twelve in the forenoon; We, for lawful causes, graciously grant this our LICENCE AND FACULTY as well to you the parties contracting, as to the Rector, Vicar, Curate, or Minister of —, the aforesaid —, who is designed to solemnise the marriage between you, in the manner and form above specified, according to the rites of the Book of Common Prayer, set forth for that purpose by the authority of Parliament.
>
> Given under the seal of our VICAR-GENERAL, this day of —, in the Year of Our Lord one thousand eight hundred and —, and in the — year of our translation.

The licence remains in force for three months only; and the copy received by the person applying for it is left in the hands of the clergyman who marries the parties, it being his authority for so doing. In case either party is a minor, the age must be stated, and the consent of the parents or guardians authorised to give such consent must be sworn to by the gentleman or lady applying for the licence. The following are the persons having legal authority to give their consent in case of minority: 1st, the father; if dead – 2nd, the guardians, if any appointed by his will; if none – 3rd, the mother, if unmarried; if dead or married – 4th, the guardians appointed by Chancery. If none of the foregoing persons exist, then the marriage may be legally solemnised without any consent whatever. The following are the official forms for this purpose:

CONSENTS REQUIRED IN CASE OF MINORS

Consent of Father

By and with the consent of A.B., the natural and lawful father of B.B., the minor aforesaid.

Guardian Testamentary

By and with the consent of A.B., the guardian of the person of the said C.D., the minor aforesaid, lawfully appointed in and by the last will and testament of D.D., deceased, his (or her) natural and lawful father.

Mother

By and with the consent of A.B., the natural and lawful mother of B.B., the minor aforesaid, his (or her) father being dead, and he (or she) having no guardian of his (or her) person lawfully appointed, and his (or her) said mother being unmarried.

Guardian appointed by the Court of Chancery

By and with the consent of A.B., the guardian of the person of the said C.D., appointed by the High Court of Chancery, and having authority to consent to his (or her) marriage, his (or her) father being dead, and he (or she) having no guardian of his (or her) person otherwise lawfully appointed, or mother living and unmarried.

When no Father, Testamentary Guardian, Mother, or Guardian appointed by the Court of Chancery

That he (or she) the said A.B., hath no father living, or guardian of his (or her) person lawfully appointed, or mother living and unmarried, or guardian of his (or her) person appointed by the High Court of Chancery, and having authority to consent to the aforesaid marriage.

The previous remarks have reference only to licences for marriages about to be solemnised according to the laws of the Church of England.

Marriage of Roman Catholics or Dissenters by Licence

By the Statute 6th and 7th William IV., 17 August 1836, Roman Catholics and Dissenters who may wish to be married in a church or chapel belonging to their own denomination, can obtain a licence for that purpose from the Superintendent Registrar of the district in which one of the parties resides, after giving notice thereof a week previous to the same officer. The expense of the licence is £3 12s. 6d.

Marriage before the Registrar

Should the parties wish to avoid the expense of a licence, they can do so by giving three weeks' notice to the Superintendent Registrar; which notice is affixed in his office, and read before the proper officers when assembled; at the expiration of that time the marriage may be solemnised in any place which is licensed within their district. The Registrar of Marriages of such district must have notice of and attend every such marriage. The fee due to the Registrar of Marriages for attending the ceremony and registering the marriage (by licence) is 10s., and for certificate 2s 6d; and without a licence 5s, and certificate 2s 6d.

Marriages also by the above-mentioned Act of Parliament may, upon due notice, be celebrated in the office of the Superintendent Registrar, with or without licence, or with or without any religious ceremony; but the following declarations, which are prescribed by the Act, must be made at all marriages,

in some part of the ceremony, either religious or otherwise, in the presence
of the Registrar and two witnesses – viz.:'I do solemnly declare that I know
not of any lawful impediment why I, A.B., may not be joined in matrimony
to C.D.;' and each of the parties shall also say to each other –'I call upon
these persons here present to witness that I, A.B., do take thee, C.D., to be
my lawful wedded wife' (or husband).

It is highly to the credit of the people of this country, and an eminent proof
of their deep religious feeling, that all classes of the community have virtually
repudiated these 'Marriages by Act of Parliament;' nor would we advise any
fair maiden who has a regard to the comfort and respect of her after con-
nubial life, to consent to be married in the Registrar's back parlour, after due
proclamation by the Overseers and Poor-Law Guardians.

The Bridal Trousseau, and the Wedding Presents

The day being fixed for the wedding, the bride's father now presents her with
a sum of money for her trousseau, according to her rank in life. A few days
previously to the wedding, presents are also made to the bride by relations
and intimate friends, varying in amount and value according to their degrees
of relationship and friendship – such as plate, furniture, jewellery, and articles of
ornament, as well as of utility, to the newly-married lady in her future station.
These, together with her wedding dresses, &c., it is customary to exhibit to
the intimate friends of the bride a day or two before her marriage.

Duty of a Bridegroom-Elect

The bridegroom elect has on the eve of matrimony no little business to
transact. His first care is to look after a house suitable for his future home, and
then, assisted by the taste of his chosen helpmate, to take steps to furnish it in
a becoming style. He must also, if engaged in business, make arrangements for
a month's absence; in fact, bring together all matters into a focus, so as to be
readily manageable when after the honeymoon he shall take the reins himself.
He will do well also to burn most of his bachelor letters, and part with, it
may be, some few of his bachelor connections; and he should communicate,
in an easy informal way, to his acquaintances generally, the close approach of
so important a change in his condition. Not to do this might hereafter lead

to inconvenience and cause no little annoyance.

'We must now speak of …

Buying the Ring

It is the gentleman's business to buy the ring; and let him take especial care not to forget it; for such an awkward mistake has frequently happened. The ring should be, we need scarcely say, of the very purest gold, but substantial. There are three reasons for this: first, that it may not break – a source of great trouble to the young wife; secondly, that it may not slip off the finger without being missed – few husbands being pleased to hear that their wives have lost their wedding rings; and, thirdly, that it may last out the lifetime of the loving recipient, even should that life be protracted to the extreme extent. To get at the right size required is not one of the least interesting of the delicate mysteries of love. A not unusual method is to get a sister of the fair one to lend one of the lady's rings, to enable the jeweller to select the proper size. Care must be taken, however, that it be not too large. Some audacious suitors, rendered bold by their favoured position, have been even known presumptuously to try the ring on the patient finger of the bride-elect; and it has rarely happened in such cases that the ring has been refused, or sent back to be changed.

Having bought the ring, the bridegroom should now put it into his waist-coat-pocket, there to remain until he puts on his wedding vest on the morning of the marriage; to the left-hand pocket of which he must then carefully transfer it, and not part with it until he takes it out in the church during the wedding ceremony.

In ancient days, it appears by the 'Salisbury Manual,' there was a form of 'Blessing the Wedding Ring' before the wedding day; and in those times the priest, previously to the ring being put on, always made careful inquiry whether it had been duly blessed. It would seem to be the wish of certain clergymen, who have of late brought back into use many ceremonial observances that had fallen into desuetude, to revive this ancient custom.

Who should be Asked to the Wedding

The wedding should take place at the house of the bride's parents or guardians. The parties who ought to be asked are the father and mother of the gentleman, the brothers and sisters (their wives and husbands also, if married), and indeed the immediate relations and favoured friends of both parties. Old family friends on the bride's side should also receive invitations – the rationale or original intention of this wedding assemblage being to give publicity to the fact that the bride is leaving her paternal home with the consent and approbation of her parents.

On this occasion the bridegroom has the privilege of asking any friends he may choose to the wedding; but no friend has a right to feel affronted at not being invited, since, were all the friends on either side assembled, the wedding breakfast would be an inconveniently crowded reception, rather than an impressive ceremonial. It is, however, considered a matter of friendly attention on the part of those who cannot be invited, to be present at the ceremony in the church.

Who should be Bridesmaids

The bridesmaids should include the unmarried sisters of the bride; but it is considered an anomaly for an elder sister to perform this function. The pleasing novelty for several years past, of an addition to the number of bridesmaids varying from two to eight, and sometimes more, has added greatly to the interest of weddings, the bride being thus enabled to diffuse a portion of her own happiness among the most intimate of her younger friends. One lady is always appointed principal bridesmaid, and has the bride in her charge; it is also her duty to take care that the other bridesmaids have the wedding favours in readiness. On the second bridesmaid devolves, with her principal, the duty of sending out the cards; and on the third bridesmaid, in conjunction with the remaining beauties of her choir, the onerous office of attending to certain ministrations and mysteries connected with the wedding cake.

Of the Bridegroomsmen

It behoves a bridegroom to be exceedingly particular in the selection of the friends who, as groomsmen, are to be his companions and assistants on the occasion of his wedding. Their number is limited to that of the bridesmaids: one for each. It is unnecessary to add that very much of the social pleasure of the day will depend on their proper mating. Young and unmarried they must be, handsome they should be, good-humoured they cannot fail to be, well dressed they will of course take good care to be. Let the bridegroom diligently con over his circle of friends, and select the comeliest and the pleasantest fellows for his own train. The principal bridegroomsman, styled his 'best man' has, for the day, the special charge of the bridegroom; and the last warning we would give him is, to take care that, when the bridegroom puts on his wedding waistcoat, he does not omit to put the wedding ring into the corner of the left-hand pocket. The dress of a groomsman should be light and elegant; a dress coat, formerly considered indispensable, is no longer adopted.

Duties to be Attended to the Day before the Wedding

The bride now sends white gloves, wrapped in white paper and tied with white ribbon, to each of the bridesmaids.

The bridegroom does the same to each of the bridegroomsmen.

One portion of the wedding cake is cut into small oblong pieces, and passed by the bridesmaids through the wedding ring, which is delivered into their charge for this purpose. The pieces of cake are afterwards put up in ornamental paper, generally pink or white, enamelled, and tied with bows of silvered paper. This pleasant old custom is, however, much on the wane.

The bridegroom's 'best man' on this day must take care that due notice be sent to the clerk of the parish where the ceremony is to take place, so that the church may be got ready, and the clergyman be in attendance.

It is usual too for the bridegroom's 'best man' to make arrangements for the church bells being rung after the ceremony: the rationale of this being to imply that it is the province of the husband to call on all the neighbours to rejoice with him on his receiving his wife, and not that of the lady's father on her going from his house.

The bridegroom furnishes to the bridesmaids his list for the 'Cards' to be sent to his friends; of which hereafter.

On the evening of this day the wedding breakfast should be ornamented and spread out, as far as possible, in the apartment appropriated to it.

The bridesmaids on this evening also prepare the wedding favours, which should be put up in a box ready to be conveyed to the church on the morning of the marriage. A picturesque custom is observed in many country weddings, where the bride's friends strew her path to the church door with flowers.

V

ETIQUETTE OF A WEDDING

The parties being assembled on the wedding morning in the drawing-room of the residence of the bride's father (unless, as sometimes happens, the breakfast is spread in that room), the happy cortège should proceed to the church in the following order:

'In the first carriage, the bride's mother and the parents of the bridegroom.
'In the second and third carriages, bridesmaids.
'Other carriages with the bride's friends.
'In the last carriage, the bride and her father.

Costume of the Bride

A bride's costume should be white, or some hue as close as possible to it. Fawn colour, grey, and lavender are entirely out of fashion. It is considered more stylish for a very young bride to go without a bonnet, but for her head to be covered with only a wreath of orange blossoms and a Chantilly or some other lace veil. This, however, is entirely a matter of taste; but, whether wearing a bonnet or not, the bride must always wear a veil. If a widow, she may wear not only a bonnet, but a coloured silk dress.

Costume of the Bridegroom

Formerly it was not considered to be in good taste for a gentleman to be married in a black coat. More latitude is now allowed in the costume of a bridegroom, the style now adopted being what is termed morning dress: a frock coat, light trousers, white satin or silk waistcoat, ornamental tie, and white or grey gloves.

How the Bridesmaids should be Dressed

The bridesmaids dress generally in pairs, each two alike, but sometimes all wear a similar costume. Pink and light blue, with white pardessus or mantelets, or white with pink or blue, are admissible colours. The bonnets, if worn, must be white, with marabout feathers; but, of late, bonnets have usually been discarded, the bridesmaids wearing veils instead. The whole costume of a bridesmaid should have a very light but brilliant effect, and the *tout ensemble* of this fair bevy should be so constituted in style and colour as to look well by the side of and about the bride. It should be as the warm colouring in the background of a sun-lit picture, helping to throw into the foreground the dress of the bride, and make her prominent, as the principal person in the tableau.

Arrival at the Church

The bridegroom meets the bride at the altar, where he must take especial care to arrive in good time before the hour appointed.

Order of Procession to the Altar

The father of the bride generally advances with her from the church door to the altar, followed immediately by the bridesmaids. The father of the bridegroom, if present, gives his arm to the bride's mother if she be present, as is now usual at fashionable weddings, and goes next to the bridesmaids. The friends who have come with the wedding party proceed next in succession.

The bridegroom with his groomsmen must be in readiness to meet the bride at the altar, the bridegroom standing at the left hand of the clergyman, in the centre before the altar rails.

We have seen on some occasions the bridegroom offer the bride his left arm to lead her to the altar, but this should be avoided; for by so doing, the whole order of the procession to the altar becomes inverted, and must then be arranged as follows:

The father, or some male relative or friend, and the mother of the bride, or, if she be not present, the mother of the gentleman, or one of the oldest female relations or friends of the bride's family, are to lead the way towards the altar from the vestry.

The friends who have come with the wedding party follow next in succession.

Then come the bridesmaids and bridegroomsmen in pairs.

The bridegroom, having offered his left arm to the bride, now conducts her up the centre aisle of the church to the altar. The parties in advance file to the right and left of the altar, leaving the bride and bridegroom in the centre.

The Marriage Ceremony

The bridegroom stands at the right hand of the bride. The father stands just behind her, so as to be in readiness to give her hand at the proper moment to the bridegroom. The principal bridesmaid stands on the left of the bride, ready to take off the bride's glove, which she keeps as a perquisite and prize of her office.

It was ordered by the old Rubrics that the woman, if a widow, should have her hand covered when presented by father or friend to the priest for marriage; one of the many points by which the Church distinguished second marriages. A piece of silver and a piece of gold were also laid with the wedding ring upon the priest's book (where the cross would be on the cover), in token of dower to the wife.

The words 'I Will'

… are to be pronounced distinctly and audibly by both parties, such being the all-important part of the ceremony as respects themselves: the public delivery, before the priest, by the father of his daughter to the bridegroom, being an evidence of his assent; the silence which follows the inquiry for 'cause or just impediment' testifying that of society in general; and the 'I will' being the declaration of the bride and bridegroom that they are voluntary parties to their holy union in marriage.

The words 'Honour and Obey'

… must also be distinctly spoken by the bride. They constitute an essential part of the obligation and contract of matrimony on her part. It may not be amiss here to inform our fair readers that on the marriage of our gracious Sovereign Queen Victoria to H.R.H. the late lamented Prince Albert, her Majesty carefully and most judiciously emphasised these words, thereby manifesting that though a Queen in station, yet in her wedded and private life she sought no exemption from this obligation, and in this respect placed herself on the same level with the humblest village matron in her dominions.

This obedience on the part of the wife, concerning which there is oftentimes much serious questioning among ladies old and young, while yet unmarried, is thus finely defined by Jeremy Taylor:

It is a voluntary cession that is required; such a cession as must be without coercion and violence on his part, but upon fair inducements and reasonableness in the thing, and out of love and honour on her part. When God commands us to love Him, He means we shall obey Him. 'This is love, that ye keep my commandments; and if ye love me,' says the Lord, 'keep my commandments.' Now as Christ is to the Church, so is man to the wife; and therefore obedience is the best instance of her love; for it proclaims her submission, her humility, her opinion of his wisdom, his pre-eminence in the family, the right of his privilege, and the injunction imposed by God upon her sex, that although in sorrow she bring forth children, yet with love and choice she should obey. The man's authority is love, and the woman's love is obedience. It is modesty to advance and highly to honour them who have honoured us by making us the companions of their dearest excellencies; for the woman that went before the man in the way of death, is commanded to follow him in the way of love; and that makes the society to be perfect, and the union profitable, and the harmony complete.

The Ring

The Rubric tells us 'the man shall give unto the woman a ring, laying the same upon the book with the accustomed duty to the priest and clerk.' This latter rule is, however, not now observed, it being usual to pay the fees in the vestry; but to ensure the presence of the ring, a caution by no means unnecessary, and in some measure to sanctify that emblem of an eternal union, it is asked for by the clerk previously to the commencement of the ceremony, who advises that it be placed upon the book.

We pity the unfortunate bridegroom who at this moment cannot, by at once inserting his hand into the corner (the one most ready to his finger and thumb) of his left-hand waistcoat-pocket, pull out the wedding ring. Imagine his dismay at not finding it there! – the first surprise, the growing anxiety, as the right-hand pocket is next rummaged – the blank look, as he follows this by the discovery that his neither garments have no pockets whatsoever, not even a watch-fob, where it may lie *perdue* in a corner! Amid the suppressed giggle of the bridesmaids, the disconcerted look of the bride herself, at such a palpable instance of carelessness on the part of the bridegroom thus publicly displayed before all her friends, and the half-repressed disapprobation of the numerous circle around, he fumbles in the coat-pockets, and turns them inside-out. A further but useless search causes increased confusion and general annoyance; at length it becomes evident that the unfortunate ring has been forgotten! We may observe, however, that in default of the ring, the wedding ring of the mother may be used. The application of the key of the church door is traditionary in this absurd dilemma; and in country churches a straw twisted into a circle has been known to supply the place of the orthodox hoop of gold!

After the Ceremony

… the clergyman usually shakes hands with the bride and bridegroom, and the bride's father and mother, and a general congratulation ensues.

The Clergyman and Assistant Clergymen

The clergyman of the church is invariably invited to attend, although the ceremony may be performed by some clerical friend of the bride or bridegroom. This is called 'assisting;' other clergymen who may attend in addition, as is sometimes the case, are said also to 'assist.' But as much ridicule has fallen upon the adoption of this custom, and as the expression of 'assisting' is considered an affectation, it is much less in vogue than it was; and it is no longer usual to mention the names of any other clergymen than that of the one who performs the ceremony, and of the clergyman of the church, who should be present whether invited or not. It is, indeed, his duty to attend, and he should insist on so doing, in as much as the entry of the marriage in the parish register is supposed to be made under his sanction and authority. It should not be forgotten that the presence of an 'assisting clergyman' entails the doubling of the fees. The payment of the fees is generally entrusted to the bridegroom's 'best man,' or some other intimate friend of his.

Difference of Religion

Where the bride and bridegroom are of different religions, the marriage is usually first celebrated in the church of that communion to which the husband belongs; the second celebration should immediately follow, and upon the same day. Some, however, regard it as duly deferential to the bride's feelings that the first ceremony should be performed in her own communion. There is a notion prevalent, that in the case of a marriage between Roman Catholics and Protestants, the ceremony must necessarily be first performed in a Protestant church. This is erroneous – the order of the twofold marriage is, in a legal point of view, of no moment, so long as it takes place on the same day.

The Return to the Vestry

On the completion of the ceremony the bride is led to the vestry by the bridegroom. The bridesmaids and bridegroomsmen follow, the principals of each taking the lead; then the father of the bride, followed by the father and mother of the bridegroom, and the rest of the company.

The Registry of the Marriage

The husband signs first; then the bride-wife, for the last time in her maiden name; next the father of the bride, and the mother, if present; then the father and mother of the bridegroom, if present; next the bridesmaids and the bridegroomsmen; then such of the rest of the company as may desire to be on the record as witnesses. All the names must be signed in full. The certificate of the marriage is then handed to the bride, and should be carefully preserved in her own possession.

The Wedding Favours

Meanwhile, outside the church, as soon as the ceremony is completed –and not before, for it is regarded as unfortunate – a box of the wedding favours is opened, and every servant in waiting takes care to pin one on the right side of his hat, while the coachmen, too, ornament therewith the ears of their horses. Inside the church the wedding favours are also distributed, and a gay, gallant, and animated scene ensues, as each bridesmaid pins on to the coat of each bridegroomsman a wedding favour, which he returns by pinning one also on her shoulder. Every 'favour' is carefully furnished with two pins for this purpose; and it is amazing to see the flutter, the coquettish smiling, and the frequent pricking of fingers, which the performance of this piquant and pleas-ant duty of the wedding bachelors and ladies 'in waiting' does occasion!

The Return Home

The bridegroom now leads the bride out of the church, and the happy pair return homeward in the first carriage. The father and mother follow in the next. The rest 'stand not on the order of their going,' but start off in such wise as they can best contrive.

The Wedding Breakfast

The bride and bridegroom sit together at the centre of the table, in front of the wedding cake, the clergyman who performed the ceremony taking his place opposite to them. The top and bottom of the table are occupied by the father and mother of the bride. The principal bridesmaid sits to the left of the bride, and the principal bridegroomsman on the left of the bridegroom. It may not be unnecessary to say that it is customary for the ladies to wear their bonnets just as they came from the church. The bridesmaids cut the cake into small pieces, which are not eaten until the health of the bride is proposed. This is usually done by the officiating clergyman, or by an old and cherished friend of the family of the bridegroom. The bridegroom returns thanks for the bride and for himself. The health of the bride's parents is then proposed, and is followed by those of the principal personages present, the toast of the bridesmaids being generally one of the pleasantest features of the festal ceremony. After about two hours, the principal bridesmaid leads the bride out of the room as quietly as possible, so as not to disturb the party or attract attention. Shortly after – it may be in about ten minutes – the absence of the bride being noticed, the rest of the ladies retire. Then it is that the bridegroom has a few melancholy moments to bid *adieu* to his bachelor friends, and he then generally receives some hints on the subject in a short address from one of them, to which he is of course expected to respond. He then withdraws for a few moments, and returns after having made a slight addition to his toilet, in readiness for travelling.

In some recent fashionable weddings we have noticed that the bride and bridegroom do not attend the wedding breakfast, but after a slight refreshment in a private apartment, take their departure immediately on the wedding tour. But this defalcation, if we may so call it, of the chief *dramatis personae* of the day, though considered to be in good taste, is by no means a popular innovation, but is rather regarded as a prudish dereliction from the ancient forms of hospitality, which are more prized than ever on so genial an occasion as a marriage.

Departure for the Honeymoon

The young bride, divested of her bridal attire, and quietly costumed for the journey, now bids farewell to her bridesmaids and lady friends. A few tears spring to her gentle eyes as she takes a last look at the home she is now leaving. The servants venture to crowd about her with their humble but heartfelt congratulations; finally, she falls weeping on her mother's bosom. A short cough is heard, as of someone summoning up resolution to hide emotion.

It is her father. He dares not trust his voice; but holds out his hand, gives her an affectionate kiss, and then leads her, half turning back, down the stairs and through the hall, to the door, where he delivers her as a precious charge to her husband, who hands her quickly into the carriage, springs in after her, waves his hand to the party who appear crowding at the windows, half smiles at the throng about the door, then, amidst a shower of old slippers – missiles of good-luck sent flying after the happy pair – gives the word, and they are off, and started on the long-hoped-for voyage!

ETIQUETTE AFTER
THE WEDDING

The dress of the bride during the honeymoon should be characterised by modesty, an attractive simplicity, and scrupulous neatness. The slightest approach to slatternliness in costume, when all should be exquisitely trim from chevelure to chaussure, would be an abomination, and assuredly beget a most unpleasant impression on the susceptible feelings of the husband. He will naturally regard any carelessness or indifference in this respect, at such a time, as a bad augury for the future.

The Wedding Cards

This point of sending the cards has until recently been considered as one requiring great care and circumspection, since an omission has frequently been regarded as a serious affront. To those parties whose visiting acquaintance is wished to be kept up, on the bride's card it has been the custom until lately to add the words 'At home' on such a day. But this usage is going out of vogue.

To send cards without an address is an intimation that the parties are not expected to call except in the case of friends who reside far away, or when the marriage has taken place at a distance. In fact, the address is understood to denote 'At home,' by those who adhere to the custom; it is better, however, that those words should be put upon the cards.

A practice has grown up of late, more particularly where the circle of friends is extensive, to send invitations to such as are not called to the wedding feast to attend the ceremony at church, instead of issuing cards at all.

When this rule is observed, it is usual in notifying the marriage in the newspapers to add the words 'No Cards.'

Reception of Visitors

On the return of the wedded pair from their honeymoon trip, about a month or six weeks after the wedding, they were, until recently, expected to be 'At home;' but the formality of reception days is now generally exploded. Intimate friends, whether 'At home' cards have been issued or not, will, however, be expected to pay them a visit. But if reception days have been fixed, the bride, with her husband and bridesmaids, will sit 'at home' ready to receive those to whom cards have been sent, the bride wearing her wedding dress, and the company invited to partake of wedding cake and wine to drink the health of the bride.

Returning Visits

The bride and her husband, or, in case he may not be able to attend her, the principal bridesmaid – the last of whose official duties this is – usually return all the wedding visits paid to them. Those who may have called on the bride without having received wedding cards should not have their visits returned, unless special reason exists to the contrary, such visit being deemed an impolite intrusion.

These return visits having been paid, the happy pair cease to be spoken of as bride and bridegroom, but are henceforward styled the 'newly-married couple;' and then all goes on as if they had been married twenty years.

VII

PRACTICAL ADVICE TO A
NEWLY-MARRIED COUPLE

Our advice to the husband will be brief. Let him have up concealments from his wife, but remember that their interests are mutual; that, as she must suffer the pains of every loss, as well as share the advantages of every success, in his career in life, she has therefore a right to know the risks she may be made to undergo. We do not say that it is necessary, or advisable, or even fair, to harass a wife's mind with the details of business; but where a change of circumstances – not for the better – is anticipated or risked, let her by all means be made acquainted with the fact in good time. Many a kind husband almost breaks his young wife's fond heart by an alteration in his manner, which she cannot but detect, but from ignorance of the cause very probably attributes to a wrong motive; while he, poor fellow, all the while out of pure tenderness, is endeavouring to conceal from her tidings – which must come out at last – of ruined hopes or failure in speculation; whereas, had she but known the danger beforehand, she would have alleviated his fears on her account, and by cheerful resignation have taken out half the sting of his disappointment. Let no man think lightly of the opinion of his wife in times of difficulty. Women have generally more acuteness of perception than men; and in moments of peril, or in circumstances that involve a crisis or turning-point in life, they have usually more resolution and greater instinctive judgment.

We recommend that every husband from the first should make his wife an allowance for ordinary household expenses – which he should pay weekly or monthly – and for the expenditure of which he should not, unless for some urgent reason, call her to account. A tolerably sure guide in estimating the amount of this item, which does not include rent, taxes, servants' wages, coals, or candles, &c., is to remember that in a small middle-class family, not exceeding four, the expense of each person for ordinary food amounts to fifteen shillings weekly; beyond that number, to ten shillings weekly for each extra person, servant or otherwise. This estimate does not, of course, provide for wine or food of a luxurious kind. The largest establishment, indeed, may be safely calculated on the same scale.

A wife should also receive a stated allowance for dress, within which limit she ought always to restrict her expenses. Any excess of expenditure under this head should be left to the considerate kindness of her husband to concede. Nothing is more contemptible than for a woman to have perpetually to ask her husband for small sums for housekeeping expenses, nothing more annoying and humiliating than to have to apply to him always for money for her own private use, nothing more disgusting than to see a man 'mollycoddling' about marketing, and rummaging about for cheap articles of all kinds.

Let the husband beware, when things go wrong with him in business affairs, of venting his bitter feelings of disappointment and despair in the presence of his wife and family,– feelings which, while abroad, he finds it practicable to restrain. It is as unjust as it is impolitic to indulge in such a habit.

A wife having married the man she loves above all others, must be expected in her turn to pay some court to him. Before marriage she has, doubtless, been made his idol. Every moment he could spare, and perhaps many more than he could properly so appropriate, have been devoted to her. How anxiously has he not revolved in his mind his worldly chances of making her happy! How often has he not had to reflect, before he made the proposal of marriage, whether he should be acting dishonourably towards her by incurring the risk, for the selfish motive of his own gratification, of placing her in a worse position than the one she occupied at home! And still more than this, he must have had to consider with anxiety the probability of having to provide for an increasing family, with all its concomitant expenses.

We say, then, that being married, and the honeymoon over, the husband must necessarily return to his usual occupations, which will, in all probability, engage the greater part of his thoughts, for he will now be desirous to have it in his power to procure various little indulgences for his wife's sake which he never would have dreamed of for his own. He comes to his home weary and fatigued; his young wife has had but her pleasures to gratify, or the quiet routine of her domestic duties to attend to, while he has been toiling through the day to enable her to gratify these pleasures and to fulfil these duties. Let then, the dear, tired husband, at the close of his daily labours, be made welcome by the endearments of his loving spouse – let him be free from the care of having to satisfy the caprices of a petted wife. Let her now take her turn in paying those many little love-begotten attentions which married men look for to soothe them, let her reciprocate that devotion to herself, which, from the early hours of their love, he cherished for her, by her ever-ready endeavours to make him happy and his home attractive.

In the presence of other persons, however, married people should refrain from fulsome expressions of endearment to each other, the use of which, although a common practice, is really a mark of bad taste. It is desirable also to caution them against adopting the too prevalent vulgarism of calling each other, or indeed any person whatever, merely by the initial letter of their surname.

A married woman should always be very careful how she receives personal compliments. She should never court them, nor ever feel flattered by them, whether in her husband's presence or not. If in his presence, they can hardly fail to be distasteful to him; if in his absence, a lady, by a dignified demeanour, may always convince an assiduous admirer that his attentions are not well received, and at once and for ever stop all familiar advances. In case of insult, a wife should immediately make her husband acquainted therewith; as the only chance of safety to a villain lies in the concealment of such things by a lady from dread of consequences to her husband. From that moment he has her at advantage, and may very likely work on deliberately to the undermining of her character. He is thus enabled to play upon her fears, and taunt her with their mutual secret and its concealment, until she may be involved, guilelessly, in a web of apparent guilt, from which she can never extricate herself without risking the happiness of her future life.

Not the least useful piece of advice – homely though it be – that we can offer to newly-married ladies, is to remind them that husbands are men, and that men must eat. We can tell them, moreover, that men attach no small importance to this very essential operation, and that a very effectual way to keep them in good-humour, as well as good condition, is for wives to study their husband's peculiar likes and dislikes in this matter. Let the wife try, therefore, if she have not already done so, to get up a little knowledge of the art of ordering dinner, to say the least of it. This task, if she be disposed to learn it, will in time be easy enough; moreover, if in addition she should acquire some practical knowledge of cookery, she will find ample reward in the gratification it will be the means of affording her husband.

Servants are difficult subjects for a young wife to handle: she generally either spoils them by indulgence, or ruins them by finding fault unfairly.

At last they either get the better of her, or she is voted too bad for them. The art lies in steady command and management of yourself as well as them. The well-known Dr Clark, who was always well served, used to say:

> It is so extremely difficult to get good servants, that we should not lightly give them up when even tolerable. My advice is, bear a little with them, and do not be too sharp; pass by little things with gentle reprehension: now and then a little serious advice does far more good than sudden fault-finding when the offence justly occurs. If my wife had not acted in this way, we must have been continually changing, and nothing can be more disagreeable in a family, and, indeed, it is generally disgraceful.

An observance of the few following rules will in all probability ensure a life of domestic harmony, peace, and comfort: To hear as little as possible whatever is to the prejudice of others; to believe nothing of the kind until you are compelled to admit the truth of it; never to take part in the circulation of evil report and idle gossip; always to moderate, as far as possible, harsh and unkind expressions reflecting upon others; always to believe that if the other side were heard, a very different account might be given of the matter.

In conclusion, we say emphatically to the newly-wedded wife, that attention to these practical hints will prolong her honeymoon throughout the whole period of wedded life, and cause her husband, as each year adds to the sum of his happiness, to bless the day when he first chose her as the nucleus round which he might consolidate the inestimable blessings of HOME.

> How fair is home, in fancy's pictured theme,
> In wedded life, in love's romantic dream!
> Thence springs each hope, there every spring returns,
> Pure as the flame that upward heavenward burns;
> There sits the wife, whose radiant smile is given—
> The daily sun of the domestic heaven;
> And when calm evening sheds a secret power,
> Her looks of love imparadise the hour;
> While children round, a beauteous train, appear,
> Attendant stars, revolving in her sphere.

(Holland's 'Hopes of Matrimony'.)

How to Dress Well

I

INTRODUCTION

No one disputes the fact that, when our first parents were placed in the garden of Eden, they wore no clothes. It was not until after they had acquired the knowledge of good and evil that they turned their attention to the subject of dress, which is now the engrossing thought and care of the majority.

There are still to be found amongst the uncivilised races those who are contented with as small an amount of clothing as satisfied the first inhabitants of Eden. Yet many of these show that they study personal appearance quite as much as the most fashionable of Parisian belles; for they bestow much labour, time, and thought, and endure much actual suffering in the elaborate patterns with which they tattoo, and, as they vainly suppose, embellish their faces and persons. The ancient Britons, who painted themselves in various devices, also bore witness to the natural craving after personal adornment, which seems to be inherent in the whole human race.

The particular modes in which this craving exhibits itself seem to depend upon climate and civilisation. Climate prescribes what is absolutely necessary; civilisation, what is decent and becoming. In some countries it is necessary to protect the body, and especially the head, from the power of the sun; in others, to guard it against extreme cold; while many of the savage tribes, inured to the scorching rays of the sun, almost entirely dispense with clothing, and yet have certain conceits and vanities which show that personal appearance is not disregarded. The most hostile intentions have been averted, and imminent peril escaped, by the timely present of a few rows of bright-coloured beads, or a small piece of looking-glass; and the most trumpery European gewgaws have elicited more admiration, afforded greater pleasure, and effected more goodwill, than the most costly treasures could purchase among civilised nations. A love of finery seems to belong to human nature. There is an attraction in bright and showy colours which the uncivilised cannot resist, and which is equally powerful among those who are civilised, though education and other causes may qualify it.

When we hear persons loudly declaiming against dress as a needless waste of time and money – when we hear them sighing for the return of the good old times when it was not so much considered, we are tempted to inquire at what period in the history of the world those times occurred; for we cannot learn that it was, at any time, considered to be an unimportant item of expenditure or thought. We do not by any means affirm that it may not occupy too much care; that there may not be instances in which it is suffered to engross the mind to the detriment of other things more worthy of consideration; that it may not lead to frivolity and extravagance. All this may be, and no doubt often is, true. It is quite possible, and more than probable. But we also maintain that it is a great mistake to come down upon it with a sweeping denunciation, and, in Quaker fashion, avow it to be all vanity, and assert that it must be trodden out of thought and eye. Even the Quakers themselves, who affect such supercilious contempt for dress, are very particular about the cut of their headgear, about the shade of their greys and their drabs and their browns, and, in their scrupulous neatness, show that they think as much of a grease-spot or a stain as many a damsel does of the ribbon in her cap or the set of her collar and cuffs. So that, after all, whatever professions people may make, human nature and human wants are always the same.

It by no means follows that a person who is well dressed thinks a great deal about it, or devotes much time to it. To some persons it comes quite naturally. They look well in whatever they wear; and the probability is that it occupies less of their time and thoughts than many who arrive, with infinite more labour and pains, at a less pleasing result.

In submitting this manual to the public, we do not presume to do more than offer such suggestions as may promote a better style of dress, consistent with a due regard to economy. No doubt many of our suggestions will have occurred to some of our readers, and it may seem almost needless to have made them, but we know by experience in other things that maxims are often forgotten and laid aside till something occurs to revive them.

It is easy enough for the rich to be in harmony with the prevailing fashion. They have but to open their purse-strings, and pay for any of those freaks of fancy which are called fashion. To combine a good style with economy requires judgment and contrivance, or, what is generally called, management.

There are certain points which may be considered as fundamental, without which the most rigid attention to matters of dress will go for nothing. For instance, cleanliness, which according to the old proverb, is rated so high as to be placed next to godliness, is one of these, and of primary importance. The most costly attire, if unaccompanied by it, is not only valueless, but may become a positive disfigurement, while the simplest dress, combined with cleanliness, may be absolutely refreshing. There is no reason whatever why the most menial occupation should be admitted as any excuse for want of personal cleanliness. It is always easy to distinguish between accidental dirt which cannot always be avoided, and that which is habitual.

When it is considered that the object of nine-tenths of womankind is that they may marry and settle in life, as their fathers and mothers have done before them, it is very natural that they should endeavour to make themselves as captivating as they can; only let them all bear this in mind, let their rank and station be what it may, that no man is caught by the mere display of fine clothes. A pretty face, or good figure, may captivate; but fine clothes, never. Though it is said that fine feathers make fine birds, yet no male will be caught by a trimming or a flounce.

To what end then should attention be given to dress? Why should it be made of so much consequence as to write a manual upon it? Because it is one of beauty's accessories; because as dress of some kind is absolutely necessary and indispensable, it is better that people of all classes should dress well rather than ill, and that, when it is done, it should be done sensibly and reasonably; without carelessness on the one hand, and without extravagance on the other. When we may, why should we not choose the best and most becoming? Why are we to mortify ourselves and annoy our friends by choosing something because it is especially hideous? No law, human or divine, enjoins us to disfigure ourselves.

II

TASTE IN DRESS

In dress, as in most other things, there are two kinds of taste; good taste and bad taste. We use the word 'taste' in a sense quite distinct from 'style.' It is a disputed point whether really good taste can ever be acquired, or whether it is only inherent. We are disposed to think that, in its most perfect form, it is inborn; but that education, association, familiarity with it may, and often does, arrive at the same result. For instance, a person who has always lived on close and intimate terms with those who are conspicuous for their good taste, becomes so familiarised with certain expressions of thoughts and ideas, habits of mind, and standard of life, that he unconsciously adopts them, views things from the same point, and walks in the same groove, quite irrespective of the natural tendencies of his own mind. Persons who have no natural gift or talent for painting, may acquire a knowledge of the art so as to pronounce with tolerable correctness of judgment upon the works of the old masters, from merely associating with those who are conversant with the subject, living amongst the pictures themselves, or from hearing discussions upon their respective merits. In fact, man is an imitative animal, and can adapt himself very readily to the circumstances by which he is surrounded, as well as acquire from others the results of their deeper research and greater experience. Living in an atmosphere where good taste prevails, it is not wonderful that he should acquire that power of discrimination by which the selection of what is becoming and harmonious is made easy.

There is no doubt that dress is a very fair index of the mind of the wearer. Who but a Widow Barnaby would wear a bright emerald green satin dress in the morning, and a bonnet profusely ornamented with large and brilliant scarlet flowers? Yet we have ourselves seen a lady, of ample dimensions and advanced years, similarly attired, and could think of nothing but one of those large gaudy macaws which are to be met with in every zoological garden. Who that had any regard for his own liberty would marry such a strong-minded, pretentious dame? Who could endure for life the vulgarity of mind that suggested such a costume for a fête in the country on a hot summer's day? There are some persons who think to overpower their neighbours by the splendour of their attire.

It is much easier to point out what offends against good taste than to say in so many words in what it consists.

Harmony of colour is essential to being well dressed. There are colours which 'swear' so awfully, that no one with any pretension to good taste would wear them; yet we not infrequently find instances of them. A yellow gown has been worn with a bright green bonnet; red and green, like our friend à-la-macaw; salmon colour and blue; yellow and red; green and blue. Two ill-assorted shades of the same colour, such as a dark and light blue; or a red lilac and a blue lilac; or a rose pink and a blue pink; or drab and yellow. Instances might be multiplied without end of incongruous inharmonious blending of colours, the mere sight of which is enough to give anyone a bilious fever. There are colours which, in themselves, may be inoffensive, but of which only particular shades assort well together. Blue and pink was a very favourite combination at one time; but in order to be both pleasing and effective, it must be one particular shade of each, and these softened and blended by the addition of white. Again, shades of scarlet and blue harmonize well together. Black has a wonderful power in softening down any intrusive brilliancy. It tones down scarlet and pink, blue and yellow, and gives them an indescribable charm, suggesting all kinds of pleasant things – the Cachuca and castanets, and the mantilla worn with such inimitable grace and coquetry by the Spanish ladies. Black and white is also a pleasing combination. White has generally the opposite effect of black. It adds to the brilliancy of the colours, and smartens rather than subdues. Many of those who aim at being well dressed, rarely give sufficient attention to this harmony of colour. One little thing will upset the whole. The choice of jewels or the head-dress may destroy all the effect which has been admirably conceived by an experienced dressmaker. It is on this account that some milliners prefer to supply all that is requisite for a particular costume. The man-milliner at Paris is said to be very dictatorial on this subject, and to decide very peremptorily as to what shall or shall not be worn. In morning costumes, a pair of gloves badly chosen will mar the effect of the whole. Imagine a lady dressed in mauve silk, with a mauve bonnet, and emerald green kid gloves! Or vice versa, in green silk, with a bonnet to match, and mauve-coloured gloves! Dark green, dark mauve, or plum coloured, dark salmon, or dark yellow gloves, are enough to spoil the most faultless costume; because they interrupt the harmony of colour; like the one string of a musical instrument, which, being out of tune, creates a discord throughout all the rest.

Variety in colour is another great defect in dress, quite apart from the question of their harmony. A multiplicity of colours, though not in themselves inharmonious, is never pleasing. It fatigues the eye, which cannot find any repose where it is disturbed by so many colours. A bonnet of one colour, a gown of another, with trimmings of a third, a mantle of a fourth, and a parasol of a fifth colour, can never form a costume that will please the eye. It is laid to the charge of English people, that they are especially fond of this kind of dress, whereas a French woman will dress much more quietly, though, by no means, less expensively; but in her choice of colours she will use very few, and those well assorted. For instance, a grey gown and a white bonnet, relieved by a black lace shawl or velvet mantle, indicate a refinement which may be looked in vain where the colours of the rainbow prevail. Among well dressed persons it will be found that quiet colours are always preferred. Whatever is gaudy is offensive, and the use of many colours constitutes gaudiness. Birds of gay plumage are sometimes brought forward to sanction the use of many bright colours. They are indeed worthy of all admiration; so also are flowers, in which we find the most beautiful assortment of colours; but nature has shaded and blended them together with such exquisite skill and delicacy, that they are placed far beyond the reach of all human art; and we think they are, to use the mildest terms, both bold and unwise who attempt to reproduce in their own persons, with the aid of silks or satins, the marvellous effect of colours with which nature abounds. And yet it may be observed in nature, how gay colours are neutralised by their accessories; how the greens vary in tone and tint according to the blossoms which they surround. The infinite shades and depths of colour with which nature is filled render it impossible for anyone to attempt to imitate it beyond a certain point of general harmony. This is now more generally understood than it used to be; but still we often stumble across some glaring instance in which a gaudy eye and taste have been allowed to run riot, and the result has been the reproduction of something not very unlike a bed of tulips.

It is in a host of little things such as these that good taste lies, and shows itself. We remember an instance of a lady, who was conspicuous among her fellows for her exquisitely good taste in dress, being severely commented upon by two showily-dressed women, who were the wives of wealthy merchants in one of our great seaport-towns. This lady appeared in church quietly dressed in black, with a handsome Indian shawl, of which the colours were subdued and wonderfully blended. The two representatives of the 'nouveaux riches' looked at the lady and then at each other; they turned up their noses, and shrugged their shoulders, and gave vent to their feelings, as they came away from church, in loud exclamations of disdain: 'Well! did you ever?' 'No! I never did; and she a lady too!' For their part they would be ashamed to wear such a shabby old shawl. The shawl was worth about its weight in gold; but because it was not showy, it found no favour in their eyes.

As it is so intricate a matter, and one of which a very slight thing can turn the scales, it is not easy to lay down rules by which good taste may be acquired. But there are instances of bad taste which can be avoided, and among them there is one which is self-evident, and does not relate either to harmony or to variety of colours. We allude to the good taste of dressing according to our means and station.

There is an impression in the minds of some persons, that fine feathers make fine birds, and that the world in general thinks more or less of them according to the dress they wear. Therefore, in order that they may impose upon their neighbours by their outward appearance, and, as children say, make-believe that they are richer than they really are, they dress beyond their means, and, at the cost of much privation of even the necessaries of life, make a display which they are not warranted in making. We have known those who have pinched themselves till they have brought on actual illness, or have laid the foundation of a fatal disease, in order that they might dress themselves in a style beyond their position in life. In France this is often the case. A lady who, in her ordinary attire, is as slovenly and as shabbily dressed as almost the very beggar in the street, will appear at some evening party most exquisitely dressed, and will carry on her back the savings acquired by months and years of penurious self-denial.

We respect those who struggle hard to maintain their hereditary position, and reverence within certain limits the spirit of endurance which bears in privacy the changes of fortune in order to keep up a becoming appearance in the eyes of the world. But we have no sympathy for those who, having no such excuse, having no high lineage, and to whom fortune has not been unkind, stint and screw that they may impose upon their neighbours with the notion that they are better off than they really are – better off in money, and better off in position. Imposture of this kind we confess we have no patience for. We are very intolerant of it. It is a vulgarity which, wherever it may be found, is most offensive. We go even further still, and are disposed to blame all who, whatever their circumstances or condition may have been or may be, dress beyond their means. It is possible that some relics of past grandeur may yet remain to be worn on state occasions. With that no one can quarrel; but it is a mistake to make great and unwarrantable sacrifices in order to replenish the exhausted wardrobe on its former scale of magnificence. It is better far to accept fate, to comply with the inevitable, and not waste time and strength in fighting against the iron gates of destiny. No one, whose esteem is worth having, will respect us less because we dress according to our means, even if those means should have dwindled into insignificance. But if we toil unduly to make ourselves appear to be something that we are not, we shall earn contempt and reap disappointment. It is far more noble-minded to bid farewell to all our greatness, than to catch greedily at any of the outlying tinsel that may remain here and there. This indicates good taste more than anything. To be what we are, really and simply, and without pretension, is one of the greatest proofs of good feeling which, in matters of dress, resolves itself into good taste.

There is nothing more hateful than pretension. The fable of the 'Frog and the Bull' illustrates the absurdity of it. Yet it is of everyday occurrence, and we continually meet with instances of it. Persons in humble class of life will often ape their betters, dressing after them, and absolutely going without necessary food in order to get some piece of finery. Fine gowns of inconvenient length, expanded over large crinolines – silk mantles richly trimmed – often conceal the coarsest, scantiest, and most ragged under-clothing. We have seen the most diminutive bonnets, not bigger than saucers, ornamented with beads and flowers and lace, and backed up by ready-made 'chignons,' on the heads of girls who are only one degree removed from the poor-house. Servant-girls who can scarcely read, much less write, who do not know how to spell their names, who have low wages, and, as little children, had scarcely shoes to their feet, who perhaps never saw fresh meat in their homes, except at Christmas, when it was given them by some rich neighbour, spend all their earnings on their dress, appear on Sundays in hats and feathers, or bonnets and flowers, and veils and parasols, and long trailing skirts, which they do not care to hold up out of the dirt, but with which they sweep the pavement. Can it be said that this is good taste? Assuredly not. It could not well be worse.

The question of station and of means does not seem to rule the world in general. Everything is considered to be suited to everybody; and the maid-of-all-work does not hesitate to copy, to the utmost extent of her power, the dress of the greatest lady in the land. She does not see why she should not dress as she likes, and is not restrained in her wish by good taste. We do not wish to argue in favour of any monopoly, but we confess that we should like to see people of all classes regulated by good taste in matters of dress.

On the Continent we find the evils we complain of partially remedied by national costumes; but these are fast diminishing, and are only to be found in all their perfection in those parts into which the railways have not yet penetrated. Yet, who does not look with pleasure upon the clean white cap of the French servant, or bonnet, who goes to market and to church without a bonnet, and with only her thick snow-white cap? Who does not delight in the simplicity of dress which the French, Norman, and Breton peasants still preserve? Contrast it with the dress of our servant-girls, with their crinoline and absurd little bonnets, and say which is the best taste.

After all that can be said there is no doubt that one of the objects of dress should be to enable people to do what they have to do in the best, the most convenient, and the most respectable manner. At all events it should not interfere with their occupation. Did our readers ever see a London housemaid cleaning the doorsteps of a London house? It is a most unedifying sight. As the poor girl kneels and stoops forward to whiten and clean the steps her crinoline goes up as her head goes down, and her person is exposed to the gaze of policemen and errand-boys, who are not slow to chaff her upon the size and shape of her legs. Can this be called dressing in good taste? Would it not be wiser to discard the crinoline altogether till the day's work is done, and the servants make themselves tidy for their tea and their evening recreation. In some families this is insisted on. But, on the other hand, it is complained against as an infringement upon the liberty of the subject, which is an unreasonable complaint, as the subject may go elsewhere if she dislikes to have her liberty so interfered with.

Good taste in dress is a question which is, by no means, above the consideration of old and elderly women. There are some who never can imagine themselves old. Whether it is owing to the eternal youth of their mind and spirits, or to their vanity, we do not pretend to say; but one thing is certain that again and again have we been both amused and disgusted by the way in which old women dress themselves. A lady with whom we were acquainted used to dress in blue or white gauze or tarlatan, or any light material she could lay her hands on, when she was past eighty, and she vainly imagined that, with an affectation of youth in her gait, and with the aid of the rouge-pot, she could conceal her age. She would trip into the room like a young girl, with her light gossamer dress floating around her as if she were some sylph in a ballet. She was a wonderful woman for her age, and, no doubt, had been so accustomed to the remarks that were continually made upon her agility and appearance, that she had at last grown to think herself almost as young as she was sixty years ago. It was but the other day that we saw an old woman with grey hair wearing a little hat placed coquettishly upon her head, with a large chignon of grey hair filling up the back! Sometimes we have seen old women spurning the sober tints which accord with their years, and coming out dressed like Queens of the May in garlands and flowers; and wearing bonnets that would be trying even to a belle of eighteen. But when people resolutely refuse to accept the fact that they are no longer young, it is not surprising that they should run into some extremes, and offend against good taste by dressing in a style utterly unsuited to their years. And yet there is no more pleasing sight than a good-looking old woman, who is neither afraid or ashamed to recognise the fact of her age, and wears the quiet and sober colours which belong to her years, modifying the fashion of the day to suit herself, that she may neither ape the young nor affect to revive in her own person the fashions of by-gone days. Affectation of all kinds is detestable.

So also there are rules for the young, which, if attended to, will prevent their offending against good taste. The young are, of all people, without excuse. The freshness of youth has a beauty of its own which needs but little outward adornment. The ravages of time have not to be repaired. Youth has charms of its own, and the more simply it is attired the better. Everything is in favour of the young. When they adopt elaborate or rich toilets, when they make flower-gardens of their heads, or wear strong and glaring colours, the chances are that they disfigure themselves. A young girl should never make herself conspicuous by her dress. Let it be as good as she pleases, as costly as she can afford, still let it be simple and unobtrusive. Let the general effect be pleasing and grateful to the eye; but at the same time let it be impossible to say in what it consists, or to remember her on account of any peculiarity in it. If she is beautiful, let her dress aid her beauty by not drawing away the attention from it. If she is plain, let her not attract all eyes to her plainness. Let not people say of her, 'Did you see that ugly girl with that scarlet feather in her hat?' or, 'with that bonnet covered with pearl beads, contrasting with her dark and sallow complexion?' or, 'with that bright green gown, which made her look so bilious?'

It is in small things, as well as in great, that good taste shows itself. Well-fitting gloves and boots, things of small moment in themselves, tell of a neat and refined taste. Quiet colours, well assorted; an absence of glare and display, nothing in extremes, betoken a correct eye and good taste.

It is, then, in the harmony of colour; in the use of a few colours at one and the same time; in dressing according to their means, according to their station, as well as according to their age, that people may be said to show their good taste in dress. There are, doubtless, other points of detail which will suggest themselves to the minds of our readers; but we are confident that, if attention is given to the points which it has been our wish to place prominently before them, there will be fewer of those startling peculiarities and eccentricities which offend against good taste.

III

FASHION IN DRESS

It is very difficult to say what constitutes Fashion. We allow our French neighbours to prescribe what we shall wear, and at certain seasons of the year, English milliners of any pretension flock to Paris to learn their lesson, and on their return to London, announce to the public and to their customers that they are prepared to exhibit the greatest novelties in style, form, and colour, which they have been able to procure. The variety that is presented, as having been just imported from Paris, convinces us that there exists everywhere, even in the great French capital itself, the greatest possible diversity of taste; and, if we may judge from the extraordinary specimens which are introduced to our notice, we should infer that the Parisian taste is by no means faultless.

We do not mean to insinuate that a really well-dressed Frenchwoman is not better dressed than most English women, or that the French have not a peculiar knack of putting on their clothes to the best advantage; for there is no doubt upon the matter. But, if we may be allowed to judge from the examples brought over to us in the shape of bonnets and head-dresses, and other articles of a lady's toilette, we should say that there must be a considerable inclination among our foreign neighbours to what is both gaudy and vulgar.

When anyone complains to a milliner of the style of any of the articles she has on sale, she replies that she is obliged to provide for all kinds of taste; that it would not answer her purpose to limit her supply to those who have a faultless eye; that, in order to make her business succeed, she must be prepared to accommodate all persons, and cater for them all alike, studying to please each individual in whatever way she may be disposed to be pleased, and never presuming to do more than merely suggest some slight improvement or modification. Ladies are apt to take offence at their taste being too severely criticised, and dressmakers do not always find it the easiest possible task to steer clear between securing their own reputation as 'artistes' of fashion and good taste, and avoiding giving offence to their patronesses. It is the public who are to blame. When someone remonstrated with Braham for his florid and vulgar style of singing, he replied, it was the people and not he who was at fault. It was alike his duty and interest to please the public, and not to instruct it. He sang to be listened to and encored, not to be hissed and snubbed. It does not answer for any tradesman not to be able to supply what his customers demand.

It is the public who are to blame. If they insist upon being supplied with certain articles of consumption or of dress, the shopkeepers have no alternative but to supply them. If ladies prefer what is ugly and misbecoming, the dressmakers have to make it. It is the old story over again of the demand creating the supply.

There will always be persons who do not know how to dress well; who have ideas of their own to which they are determined to give expression. When they think they are doing their best, and are bent upon astonishing the world, they somehow appear to the worst advantage. They endeavour to rival their neighbours in strength and variety of colours; and, if they see a beautiful woman becomingly dressed, they at once copy that woman, quite regardless of their personal appearance, which may be the least fitted to the style which has taken their fancy. It reminds us of the story of a fashionable shoemaker, who, having made a pair of shoes for a lady who was remarkable for the beautiful shape of her foot, was applied to by another lady to make her a pair exactly similar to Lady So and So's. The shoemaker looked with dismay at his new customer's foot, which bore no resemblance whatever to that of her friend. At last he looked up at the lady, shrugged his shoulders, shook his head, and said: 'Madam, it is impossible; you must bring me a foot like her ladyship's before I can make a shoe like hers.' The rebuke was well deserved: but his honesty lost him a good customer.

The assortment and choice of colours, though chiefly a matter of taste, is yet under the direction of fashion. At one time one colour predominates, at another time another; while two colours may be used together at one time, which at another are almost interdicted.

There is nothing more capricious, more inexplicable, more wayward, than fashion. It is true that, taken as a whole, there is a certain conformity in the rules it prescribes. For instance, as the crinoline diminishes in size and the area which petticoats cover in their circumference is lessened, so also bonnets have grown smaller, and the enormous plait of hair which has taken the place of the chignon, keeps in countenance the extraordinary length of ladies' trains.

If anyone cares to be amused she might investigate the fashions of by-gone days. The transitions are wonderful, and do not appear to be guided by any rule. Those of the gentlemen are simply absurd. Since the days of Van Dyck, there has been nothing attractive in their dress; nothing pictur-esque. It has been as ugly as possible, and continues to be so. The nearest approximation to anything less hideous than the present fashion is in the 'knickerbockers,' which are generally worn by sporting men and pedestrians – men who shoot, or who are addicted to walking tours. There was an attempt on the part of one or two individuals to introduce them, by means of velvet and silk hose, for evening wear; but the example was not followed, and the swallow-tailed coat still prevails.

In order to dress strictly according to fashion, and to comply with the ever-changing caprice, it is necessary to have a large and well-filled purse, and a wardrobe that is not too extensive; because, as the fashion varies with almost every season, a large number of dresses involves either a great and needless waste of money, or the necessity of always being a little behind the fashion of the day. Besides which, as this capricious goddess has prescribed what shall be worn for driving, for walking, for morning, noon, and night; and demi-toilettes and full-dress toilettes have each their own peculiarities, it really becomes a very serious item of expenditure for such ladies as make it the business of their lives to follow the fashions of the day.

Fashion prescribes rules for all. All classes of society bow, more or less, to her decrees. The fine lady who frequents the Court, as well as the servant-girl who sweeps out the area of a London lodging-house, and all the intermediate classes, are guided by Fashion. Crinolines and bonnets prove this, as well as the length of the skirts which are suffered to trail along in all the dirt and dust of pavement and crossings. It always takes some time before a fashion which has been adopted by the higher orders prevails among the lower; but, if it is a fashion which survives beyond the moment, it invariably finds its way downward in the course of time. Fashion prescribes the size and shape of bonnets, the make of gowns, their length and their size – the number of breadths and gores – the trimmings, the petticoats, which have become like a second gown, and all the other paraphernalia of a lady's toilette. There is no part of a lady's dress too minute for her inspection and care and legislation. The colour of gloves, the dye of hair, the application of false hair, the make of boots and shoes, the choice of ornaments, are all ordered and arranged.

Fashion is a sort of 'act of uniformity,' which would bring all flights of fancy within certain prescribed limits. It defines the boundaries within which ladies may safely indulge their own conceits.

The best-dressed persons are not always those who are led blindfold by the prevailing fashion, nor by any means those who are strong-minded enough to defy it, and set it at nought. Anyone who defies the fashion of the day, and, when long skirts and small saucer-like bonnets prevail, dares to walk abroad with very short petticoats, which she holds up unnecessarily high; displaying a foot and ankle that had better be hidden out of sight; who spurns a crinoline, and therefore looks like a whipping post; who wears a many-coloured shawl because cloaks and mantles are the rage; who adorns her head with a bonnet that is of the coal-scuttle cut, over which she fastens a large, coloured gauze veil, because she desires to protest, as far as she can, against the innovations of fashion; such a one will never attract, nor influence the public mind. She will provoke a smile, but will never recommend her own peculiar and independent style of dress. And she who follows fashion like a slave, wears what is prescribed without regard to her own personal appearance; who considers neither her age, nor her figure, nor her station, nor her means; who simply allows herself to be an advertisement for the milliner she employs, will often appear eccentric, and generally ill-dressed.

It is never sufficiently considered that everyone has her 'points,' and that nothing so much offends as discrepancies. We remember a discussion upon female beauty, when instances were brought forward of persons who were conspicuous for their good looks, but who could not boast of one really perfect feature. The effect of the *tout ensemble* was good, and most attractive, but when the faces were pulled to pieces, it was impossible to say in what the beauty consisted. One of the critics wisely said, that it was to be found in the perfect harmony of feature and expression. All the features were on the same scale; no one feature overpowered the other, and the expression called into activity all features alike, so that there was perfect unity and harmony throughout. To compare small things with great, we should say that this supplies a good rule for dressing well. There should be no discrepancies. It should be harmonious, not only in itself, but harmonious with the person whom it is intended to adorn. It should be in keeping with face and figure. No two persons are exactly alike. Every one has her 'points,' which constitute her beauty and her charm; and these 'points' have to be attended to carefully. A woman who does this, with due regard to the rules of fashion, will always be well dressed. She will not buy or wear a thing simply because it has 'just come from Paris,' nor be influenced by milliners and shopmen who assure her that the ugly article they exhibit is original in shape and style. Though fashion dictates, and she follows, yet she follows in a way of her own. She is never behind fashion, and never in advance of it. Perhaps her most admired 'toilette' has been made at home, under her own eye, which has directed how far a compliance with the prevailing fashion suits her. She does not startle the world with a combination of strange colours, nor entertain her friends with a peculiarity of style and make. What she wears is prettily arranged, well made and well put on, and the effect is both pleasing and refreshing, and people inquire what house in Paris she patronises. She is prudent; and, keeping her own secret, does not offend the fastidiousness of her fashionable friends by letting the truth eke out, that her much-admired Parisian 'toilette' is, in every sense, of home-produce, but smiles at their approval, and follows her own plan, which is so successful in its results. Her costume is not expensive, and she contrives that, whatever she wears shall not offend against the laws of Fashion, while she declines to be its slave. She is not addicted to sham jewellery; she has no weakness for tinsel. What she wears is good of its kind, even when it is not costly. Wherever she goes, she impresses everyone with the fact that she is a true gentle-woman. She knows what is suited to her station and age, and, without conceit, understands what are her 'points.' She is well aware that no woman can afford to be indifferent to her personal appearance, and that no law, human or divine, requires her to disfigure herself. A married woman has to bear in mind that she must dress not only to please her husband, but also to reflect credit upon his choice. The unmarried to impart to herself as prepossessing an appearance as will be likely to attract the opposite sex. Neither before or after marriage can any woman neglect her person with impunity. Nor can she set her face entirely against the fashions of the day. She may modify them to suit herself, and to bring out her 'points;' but she cannot safely disregard or defy them.

Fashion gives, as it were, the key-note – supplies the hint, which is taken and followed as people can. It is absurd to suppose that its laws are stringent, and not elastic, or that all persons must conform exactly to its 'dicta.' Who shall say that all must dress alike? Tall and short, fat and lean, stout and scraggy, cannot be made equally subject to the same rule. In such a matter as dress there must be some margin allowed for individual peculiarities. Nature has not made us all in the same mould; and we must be careful not to affront nature, but must accept her gifts and make the best of them.

There is one point connected with the following of fashion which requires some attention, and which, if attended to, will preserve us from incongruities. We allude to the disposition of some persons to use various fashions together. They are inclined to be 'eclectic.' They select from by-gone fashions, and endeavour to blend them with those which prevail. The result is a painful incongruity. Who would dream of placing a Grecian portico to an Elizabethan building? Why then endeavour to combine old fashions with new? Why attempt to wear a bonnet of almost primitive form with dresses of modern dimensions and style? or why wear flounces when they are out of fashion, and full skirts when everything is 'gored' into plainness? It is necessary to pay some attention to the present style of dress, if ladies desire to avoid peculiarities and wish to please. But it, of course, requires a certain sense of propriety and of fitness. A bonnet of diminutive form which suits to perfection a young girl with a small oval face and slender throat, is quite misapplied when adopted by a woman of a certain age, whose figure has escaped beyond the limits of even 'embonpoint,' whose throat is not perceptible, and whose face and head are large. She requires something of more ample dimensions, that bears some affinity in size with the head and face it is intended to ornament; something which will modify, if not conceal, the imperfections which time has developed. A dress of a light and airy kind does not become a matron; nor can that which suits a slight and elastic figure be worn with impunity by what is called a 'comely dame.'

Fashion prescribes all sorts of rules about breadths, gores, flounces, and such like, and these are the hints which she gives, and which ladies must take and apply to themselves to the best advantage. There is ample margin allowed for each one to adopt what is best suited to her own particular style of beauty. Perhaps there never was a time when so much liberty was allowed to ladies to dress according to their own fancy. Of course we mean within certain limits. If anyone will consent to keep within those limits, and not do actual violence to the decrees of fashion, she may, to a considerable degree, follow her own fancy. If the general idea which fashion has submitted to society as the *sine qua non* of being well dressed is borne in mind, she is very tolerant of the various modifications which ladies, for the most part, wisely adopt, that they may not make 'guys' of themselves. Nothing illustrates this more than the hats and bonnets which are worn. Their variety is so great that their names might be termed 'legion;' and a pretty woman may adopt all kinds of conceits, providing she neither offends the eye nor defies the prevailing fashion. One may come out as a shepherdess, another like a Spanish cavalier in the time of

Charles II, another with a three-cornered hat such as state-coachmen wear on 'drawing-room days,' only of course a very small edition of it; another with a little coquettish hat that suggests one of Watteau's most successful pictures; but no one may wear one of those large mushroom bonnets which were worn some five-and-thirty years ago, and which were ornamented by large bows of ribbon stiffened with wire, and by great nosegays of flowers which resembled a garden flower-pot. It is only on condition that no violence is done to the decrees of fashion or to the ideas she would suggest, that so much liberty is allowed. We think that the result is most satisfactory, as there is an infinite variety to please the eye, and there are abundant opportunities for everyone to attend to her own comfort and ease. Of course there have been, and still are, certain fashions which are quite *de rigueur* among the really fashionable world, and which are annoying to the public generally, such as large crinolines and long skirts, and more especially the long trains which are now in vogue. Crinolines, though reduced in size, are not discarded, except in some instances which, as our eyes are not yet accustomed to their absence, present a scarcely decent appearance.

One word more before we close this division of our subject. If persons are inclined to rail against Fashion and denounce it, let them remember that there is a fashion in everything. In thought, in politics, in physic, in art, in architecture, in science, in speech, in language, and even in religion we find fashion to have a guiding and governing power. How can we otherwise account for the change which has taken place in language, which is not the same that it was fifty years ago? There are phrases which have become obsolete; there are words which have been almost lost out of our vocabulary, which have changed their meaning, or which fashion has tabooed. And in other matters we find alterations which can only be accounted for by the fact that fashions change. They are not the result of development simply, which may and must frequently occur in sciences; but they are the result of those variations in custom and usage for which it is impossible to find any more expressive word than that of Fashion. Why then should not dress have its fashions also, and why should not those fashions change as time advances, and why should not fashion rule in this as in other things?

IV

EXPENSE OF DRESS

This is a portion of our subject which awakens the liveliest interest in persons of both sexes. It is the complaint of many men of our times that the dress of women is a very costly affair. The complaint is often made apparently under a sense of wrong, as if they had been made to suffer from it. Some time ago considerable attention was directed to the subject by some letters which appeared in one of the leading journals of the day, in which grave reflections were made upon the exceeding costliness of dress at the present time. It was said to exceed that of any former age, and to be the reason why so many young men flinch from the idea of matrimony. Among these requirements dress occupies a prominent place. The style and variety of dress which is affirmed to be necessary for young ladies in the highest grade of society renders it no easy matter for them to find men both qualified and willing to afford them sufficient funds to procure what custom had created into a necessity. It may be owing to the quantity of material which the dressmakers require in order to make a dress, as well as to the variety which fashion has prescribed. At all events, let people say what they may, we believe that there is no doubt whatever that the expense of dress has become very much greater than it was thirty years ago. A dressmaker could then make a very first-rate gown, suited to any function at Court or elsewhere, for ten or twelve pounds, whereas now the most ordinary gown, suitable to wear only at a family dinner-party, cannot be made for less than fourteen or fifteen pounds. A ball gown will cost eighteen or twenty pounds; and in Paris a thousand francs, (forty pounds,) is considered nothing out of the way; and evening and ball dresses often cost two thousand francs each. It is not surprising then that, if this is the ordinary expense of a lady's dress, men should hesitate before they embark in matrimony, and add so large an item to their expenditure. We remember to have heard it said that five hundred a year pin-money was a very small allowance for a young married woman; that it would require the most wonderful management to enable her to dress well and keep within her income. Of course everyone knows that there are many women who dress upon infinitely less; but we are speaking of those who profess to dress well, and whose position in society requires them to be well dressed.

What then is the reason why dress has become so expensive? Is it because the materials which are in use are costly, or is it because the needlewomen are better paid, and, wages being higher, dressmakers' charges are also higher in proportion? We do not believe that either of these are the cause; but simply that a larger quantity is required, and that variety has become a *sine qua non*. Some years ago the cost of a silk dress was about half what it is now, not because the price of silk has increased, but because a much larger quantity is required. Perhaps of the two, silk is cheaper than it used to be; but where ten and twelve yards sufficed, twenty and twenty-three are scarcely sufficient. Then the variety that is considered indispensable adds to the cost of dress. Where three or four dresses constituted the wardrobe of many, three times that number are now considered a scanty supply. Some ladies do not like to wear the same dress twice at the same place; and, if they visit in the country, take with them luggage enough for a twelvemonth, and appear daily, and, in some instances, three times a day, in some fresh costume. It may perhaps be said that these are exceptional cases, but they are not so. Ladies-maids, servants, and even village girls have more gowns now than persons of the same class had formerly. This adds to the cost of dress, and makes it altogether a more expensive affair than it used to be. Our fore-mothers who rejoiced in farthingales had, no doubt, the most costly attire, but it lasted longer, and became the inheritance of children and children's children; besides which their wardrobes were not by any means so expensive as that of a 'grande dame' of 1875.

Materials are an important element in the matter of dress, and we propose, in the few remarks we shall make on the subject of expense, to offer some suggestions which shall tend to make it less.

In the first place every young lady is without excuse who spends a large sum annually upon her dress, for she possesses in her youth that which makes the most simple and inexpensive attire the most suitable and becoming. Everything is appropriate to youth. The freshest flowers of the garden, the plainest muslins, tarlatans and tulles do not come amiss. In the country fresh flowers are more admissible than those that are artificial. In London it is the reverse. The heat of a crowded ball-room soon makes the brightest flowers wither; besides which there would be an affectation in a young lady's making her appearance in a London ball-room decked, like the goddess Flora, with real flowers; while all the world prefer the artificial as the least troublesome and the most enduring.

For the young, cheap and inexpensive materials are often the most effective. Heavy silks and satins are out of place. It is more a question of colour and make than material. How often a bright green and white muslin, or even cotton, well made and well put on, worn by a pretty girl with a good complexion and graceful *tournure*, puts to shame and thoroughly eclipses a more costly and elaborate 'toilette!' How often we have been charmed by the appearance, at the breakfast table, of a young fresh looking girl, who in her simple and unpretending, but well-selected attire, suggests all that is most beautiful in nature, the early sunrise, the opening rose-bud, encased in its calix of tender green! Such a sight has refreshed while it has gratified the eye, and if the young only knew how very little is required to add to those charms which are the property of youth, they would not be at so much pains to copy those elaborate 'toilettes' which seem to be invented only to repair the inroads and damages of years, and to enrich the dressmakers, and which are quite *de trop*, quite out of place with the young. Many are the materials which suit the young and which are inexpensive. Alpacas of various shades, muslins, foulards, tarlatan, tulle, light silks, light in texture as well as colours. These are not expensive materials. We remember at this moment an exceedingly effective costume, made of white alpaca with a narrow green stripe, which was worn with a crinoline bonnet trimmed with mauve. The bonnet and dress did not cost more than £2 10s., and scarcely as much. It was made at home, and all that was required for the gown was nothing when compared to the bills which the most ordinary dressmaker would have run up for tapes and buttons, and hooks and eyes.

But dressmakers have their fortunes to make, and it is well for them that there are people in the world who are rich enough to employ them. Some dressmakers refuse to make up what is called 'the lady's own materials,' that is, they require their customers to buy the materials of them, and therefore it is by no means difficult to understand that, under such circumstances, a dressmaker's bill may reach any amount, and their profits become enormous.

Compared with the supplies of thirty years ago there is no doubt that the materials out of which ladies may make their selection have increased very

considerable. The variety of foulards, of gauzes, of alpacas, of camlets, of pop-
lins, poplinettes, and Japanese silks, and even of silks themselves, which vary
from three shillings to eight and nine shillings the yard, of satins, of velvets,
and velveteens, have brought dress within the scope of moderate incomes.
Each year some novelty is introduced, and a clever hit in the name given to
it makes it popular; just as that of 'Japanese silk' made people run eagerly after
a material of home manufacture, which is made of silk and cotton. There are
a host of other materials cheaper still, which may be obtained for a few shillings the dress, some of which are not by any means to be despised. With so
great a supply, it is strange that dress should be so costly; but the fact is, that
this is an age in which people are more disposed to ape their betters than to
dress according to their means. If, however, they desire to spend only a small
sum, they must take some trouble about it, and must contrive how to produce
a good result with simple and even common materials.

The great improvement in muslins and in calicoes – the good patterns
which are printed on common linens – have made it quite inexcusable for
people to dress ill. Some of the prettiest costumes that we have seen have
been made in cheap materials, and persons who have admired them have
been quite astonished to find that they have bestowed their admiration upon
an 'inferior article.'

For autumn wear there are camlets, alpacas, and serge of all colours, which
are designated 'Yachting and Sea-side Costumes,' but which are suitable for
all places. Their effect is exceedingly good, braided or otherwise. They may
be got anywhere, though Cowes boasts of having the best assortment. We
have seen white braided with black, or with a pattern printed on it in black;
blue, light and dark; brown; green braided in white, the effect of which has
been good; and we have seen scarlet, which is very trying, and more suited
for winter. It is effective when toned down with black velvet, but it looks
rather heavy and overpowering.

For winter, there are droguets, reps in worsted and in silk, merinos, tweeds,
linseys, and velveteens. We do not mention silk, because it is universally
acknowledged that there is nothing so well suited to all seasons. It looks better
than anything else, is the pleasantest to wear, and may be procured of almost
any substance. Velveteens have a very good effect – better than most materials;
and when they are braided well, they are very effective. The black looks the
best, and is the most serviceable; and when worn with a mantle, or cloak, or
jacket to match, it makes one of the best costumes for walking or driving.
The brown velveteen is effective. It is considered warm and light – two most

important qualities for clothing; for, with the amplitude of modern skirts, it is absolutely essential that materials should be light as well as warm.

For spring and summer it is needless to specify more materials than have been already named. The only point to be considered is that in spring, dress should be, in our uncertain climate, suited to changes of weather, and temperature, and should be in harmony with the season when nature is putting on her best apparel, and woods and fields become hourly more green and full of vegetation. In summer, dress should be light and cool and quiet; because, beneath a glowing sun, bright colours do not please, unless they harmonise with the blue sky or green earth.

The second important point in matters of dress is the make or cut. Upon this depends the question whether cheap materials can be worn. An ordinary stuff or calico well made, fashionably made, and well put on, is never out of place. It, not infrequently, puts to shame many richer materials which are not so well made nor so well selected.

This question of make or cut (call it which you please) is not sufficiently considered, especially by the young.

Some people think no one can be well dressed who is not expensively dressed, whose gown is not richly trimmed; but it is a great mistake. Many persons are absolutely ill-dressed who spend a fortune upon their clothes.

The young should bear in mind that simplicity is what harmonises best with youth, but care must be taken to avoid the simplicity of the school-room and of a 'miss in her teens.' We can call to mind a young lady who made her appearance at an evening party in London, where 'all the world and his wife' were collected together, and when it was necessary to be somewhat smart, in a rather skimp spotted muslin, with a black belt and a few black cherries in her hair. She looked, as the reader will easily believe, like a young lady in her teens, who, as Byron said, 'smells of bread and butter.' She was much on the wrong side of twenty. By her side stood a young girl who had not passed nineteen summers, dressed in the freshest costume of plain white tulle, with bright turquoise-blue flowers in her hair, the very impersonation of youth and loveliness. The cost of the dress of these two young ladies was about the same, but the appearance of the two was by no means the same. The one was fresh and simple; the other simple but unfresh. The one attracted; the other repelled. At the same time we saw two sisters, one a blonde and the other dark, dressed unadvisedly alike in dark blue tarlatan, with an infinite number of beads round the body, peplum, and sleeves. It was in the height of summer, and the costume looked fusty and oppressive; while not far off stood a young girl in a white and green tarlatan dress prettily trimmed with old lace and green ribbon, with one large white flower in her hair – the very type of spring and early summer. None of these costumes were expensive, but they had widely different results.

We return to our former assertion that it is the make which renders a common material wearable in any – even the very best – society.

It requires, of course, a knowledge of the prevailing fashion, which may easily be arrived at by the simple process of taking in *Le Follet*, or some good monthly publication on fashions. It requires also a correct eye and a good taste to select such materials as shall harmonise well with the style which is in favour. It requires, above all, a good workwoman, who knows how to cut out, how to put in the gores, how to arrange the breadths, where to put the fulness; where to make the dress full, and where tight, how to avoid creases, how to cut the sleeves, and how to put them in, how to give the arm sufficient room so that the back shall not pucker, how to cut the body so that short waisted ladies shall not seem to have too short a waist, nor long-waisted ladies too long a one. This important question of a good lady's maid is one upon which depends the probability of being well dressed and economically dressed. It is absolutely necessary for a person of moderate means, to whom the needless outlay of a shilling is of real importance, to make her things at home. If she cannot make them herself, she must find a clever needle-woman who has learned her business, and knows milliner's phraseology and the meaning of terms, and how to cut out to the best advantage. She will then be able to use common material, buy smaller quantities of them, and will always look well dressed. Her gown will always be ironed when it wants ironing; it will be mended whenever a stitch has broken loose; the collars and cuffs will always be clean and of the right shape and size; and no one will enquire into the quality and cost of the material of which the effect is so pleasing.

A lady's maid that is quick and efficient is the best friend a lady can have who wishes to be well dressed and at a small expense. She saves her wages again and again. But not so with a lady's maid who does not understand her business. If she is always requiring assistance, and cannot make the simplest gown without a needle-woman to help her, and will not attempt a smart dress at all, or who makes it so slow that either the occasion for which it is required slips by, or a much longer notice is necessary than the most fashionable dressmaker would demand in the very height of the London season, instead of being useful, she is an incumbrance. The dressmaker's bill is not avoided. A steady lady's maid who is quick at her needle and quick with her eye, can always command good wages and a good place, and they who possess such a treasure will never be willing to part with her. Anyone who has not thoroughly gone into the question would not believe what a saving it is to 'make at home.' It is not only that the milliner's bill is saved, but the materials which are used do not cost so much. Nor is this all, an efficient lady's maid can clean and turn and re-make dresses so as to give them the look of new. To those who have but small incomes, it is of great importance not to be under the necessity of making frequent additions to their wardrobes, and anyone who can, by good management, enable them to wear a dress longer than they otherwise would, saves them, in the end, considerable outlay.

We have heard ladies say that nothing has provoked them more than the way in which their maids can make up for themselves dresses which they have laid aside. They can, by dint of sponging and washing, and pressing, and ironing by turning, and many other ways known to them, make their ladies' cast off clothes look as good as new, and many a lady has, before now, looked with envy upon an old dress which reappears in a new character, looking quite as fresh and attractive as ever, under the magic hand of a clever and practical needle-woman.

We maintain then, that, though the present style of dress may be expensive on account of the enormous quantity of material which is required, there is no real reason why it should be so costly as it is supposed to be. If ladies will give some attention to the make or cut and style of their dresses, the most simple materials will look exceedingly effective. It only requires judgment, good taste, and some forethought and contrivance.

We recommend as of primary importance, in order to be well and economically dressed, that people of slender means should have their dresses made at home, and should secure the services of a clever needle-woman who knows how to cut out and make, and has learned the mysteries of the art of dressmaking. With her assistance there is no reason why a home-made dress should not bear comparison with those of Madame Descon of London, or of Mr Wirth of Paris. It is in the style, that first-class dressmakers excel. It is not in the actual needlework, which is often a very inferior affair. If, with the help of *Le Follet*, ladies will give some attention to the subject of dress, and will assist their maids with suggestions and approval, they will find themselves amply repaid, not only by their own personal appearance, but also by the small outlay of money.

V

ACCESSORIES

There are an infinite variety of things which are necessary in order to make a woman thoroughly well dressed, which do not come under the category of dresses. Some of these must be discussed, as they are of great importance.

To begin with bonnets. How much of a lady's toilette depends upon her bonnet! – upon its make, its shape, its style, and the materials it is made of!

In these days, bonnets are much less ugly than they formerly were. They are not set at the back of the head as they used to be, when they made every woman look as if her neck had been broken. They offered no advantage. They did not screen the face from sun and wind, and no ladies could keep them on their heads without the help of long pins like skewers. The bonnet, as now worn, scarcely deserves the name of a bonnet. It is more like a cap than a bonnet; but, such as it is, it is exceedingly becoming to the young – more especially the style which has most recently come into fashion, in which, while it ties behind, below the chignon or large plait of hair, long ends of tulle, or lace, or blonde fall round the cheek, and fasten under the chin with a brooch or a flower. The effect of the lace against the face is very preferable to that of the fold of hard ribbon which was generally worn, and which was utterly devoid of all grace. Besides which, we have heard ladies praise the last fashion as being the most comfortable, because the absence of strings fastened under the chin enables them to eat, and sing, and talk without the necessity of taking off the bonnet, or of untying it. The extreme lightness of the modern bonnet is in itself a great recommendation. But if a bonnet is intended as a protection to the head from sun, wind, and rain, then, indeed, it must be allowed that the present fashion does not fulfil any of those intentions. A small saucer of tulle, or three-cornered bit of lace ornamented with a few flowers, which fits on the head in the small space that intervenes between the front hair and the beginning of the chignon, where it stops in order that the huge mass of hair now worn at the back of the head may be fully exhibited, does not do more than make a very pretty toilette. Useful and serviceable as a protection, it is not. But when it is contrasted with bonnets which were worn a few years ago, or with those which our mothers and grandmothers wore, we confess that we are glad of the change.

No lady ought to be indifferent about her bonnet. It is to her face what the setting is to a jewel. The arrangement of the lace or blonde; the way it accords with the countenance; the harmony of colour with the rest of the dress, which in some instances it tones down by its quietness, and in others brightens and freshens by its contrast; all these are points to be considered. It is impossible not to be guided by fashion in the selection of a bonnet, and the same fashion will prescribe how it is to be trimmed, but, as a rule, we protest against beads and tinsel of all kinds. If beads must be used, they should be used sparingly. We saw a bonnet this year which was nothing but black beads, which were designated by the high-sounding name of 'black pearls.' The bonnet was heavy, and very ugly; and when we remonstrated against it, we were assured it had just arrived from Paris – as if the announcement of such a fact was, in itself, enough to silence all objections. But it had no effect upon us, for the bonnet was objectionable on every ground – on account of its weight and appearance.

In London, as it is necessary to have a succession of bonnets, which soon become discoloured and spoilt by the soot and dirt of our great metropolis, all that really signifies is that they should look fresh and clean, and in harmony with the dresses with which they are worn; and therefore it is important they should be cheap. To give three guineas and even more, and perhaps five, for a bonnet which will last for only one month is an expensive proceeding; and when it is considered that really pretty bonnets can be bought for eighteen shillings, which look quite as well as those which are more costly, they are without excuse who do not manage to have always one nice-looking bonnet for special occasions.

We have known some ladies who are clever and wise enough to make their own bonnets, and then the cost of them is about five or six shillings each. If the lady's maid is clever and handy, and knows how to make them, she will probably make them quite as well as any professed milliners. All that is required is to understand what fits and suits the person for whom the bonnet is intended. Everyone finds that one shape suits her better than another.

The next point in making a bonnet is that the 'artiste' should have a light hand, and should make it 'off-hand,' without letting it lie about to get soiled or tumbled. Things which are not expensive, but are made of common materials, should look fresh. If they have that merit, no one will examine them very closely to see whether the lace is real, or the flowers of the first quality. Satisfied with the general effect and style, no inquiries will be instituted into the cost of the materials. People are not so particular where their eye is pleased. On the contrary, where the effect is good, cheapness increases its value in the estimation of those who know that one and one make two.

No one can make bonnets, or indeed any kind of headgear, without one of those hideous figure-heads called 'blocks,' upon which the bonnet or the cap is made, without risk of injury. This is the only way in which the milliner can form any idea of the effect of her handiwork. She can turn it about to get the full, side, and back view of her performance, without touching the article in question, which, if it is mauled about ever so little, soon loses its freshness.

As we have long ago discarded the picturesque from bonnets, and the famous *chapeau de paille* has been laid aside, there is an advantage in the fact that the present style is unobtrusive; and strong-minded women who cling tenaciously to their beloved old coal-scuttle shape, and deride the present fashion, indignantly exclaiming against it, 'Call that thing a bonnet, indeed?' certainly tempts us to reply to their prejudiced and absurd reflections, 'Physician, heal thyself;' for if there is one thing more ugly than another, it is the old-fashioned bonnet with crown, curtain, and poke, to which a few old maids rigidly adhere – just as Quakeresses do to their hideous and antiquated style. There is a kind of self-righteousness in the protests of these ladies, with which we confess that we have no sympathy. We do not mean to recommend them to adopt the bonnet of a girl of eighteen, but we do advise them to conform to the fashion of the day, and wear a modified edition of the present and prevailing costume.

It is remarkable how straw always retains its hold as a material for bonnets. A straw bonnet, is, however, a more expensive article than one of tulle; but then it is more enduring, and better suited for country wear. There is also another advantage in straw: it never looks vulgar. A country lass in a bonnet of silk, or lace, or tulle, does not look one-half as well as one in a straw bonnet, neatly trimmed. Straw is becoming to persons of all ages and of every station. It makes a vulgar woman look less vulgar, and the lady more refined. Though common, it is never so in an offensive sense.

Caps have become an important item, from the fact that women of all ages wear something of the kind. The young girl who has passed from girlhood into matrimony, considers it necessary that some of those little caps made of lace and ribbons and which have such a coquettish look about them, should form part of her trousseau. She is as glad to exercise her new privilege of wearing a cap as an undergraduate is of wearing his cap and gown. It is a sign that she has passed to what she considers the higher state, although she knows that there are many high authorities for the contrary; but she remembers that 'doctors differ,' and she hails her privilege as one to which she has been always taught to look forward.

What can be more becoming than some of those jaunty caps which seem to mock at age? Here, again, we have a manifest improvement in the head-gear of ancient times.

Think of the turbans, the gigantic hats and caps of blonde which were made to stand erect by means of wire, and which surrounded the face like fans at full stretch, or (more gracious simile) like the nimbus round the head of a medieval saint.

Contrast these with the little caps which ornament the head with lace, as only lace can ornament it, and you will see at once how superior the present fashion is. It is not only that these pretty and mysterious fabrics of lace and ribbon are an ornament to the loveliest and most youthful; but they have worked a revolution in the caps of elderly ladies. Instead of the cap with its frill of blonde intermixed with narrow ribbon or small flowers, fitting close to the face like a fringe and tying under the chin, we see small and becoming head dresses of lace, which sufficiently furnish the cheeks and cover the hair. Where it can be done, the cap of the most elderly woman should appear to dress and furnish her head rather than her face, though, if need be, it can be made to soften the asperities of age where they have marked the countenance.

Mantles or cloaks are a difficult question.

When everybody of every station wears a cloak or mantle we are disposed to recommend shawls, especially as a really good Indian shawl cannot be imitated, and denotes the quality and condition of the wearer. Every servant girl, every maid of all work, has her Sunday cloak. None but the rich can sport an Indian shawl. It requires falling shoulders and a tall and graceful figure. It should not be fastened round the throat as if the wearer suffered from a severe cold in her throat; but it should have the appearance of being loosely put on;

neither fastened tightly on, nor falling off. Square shawls are always more ugly than not. If the wearer has not a very erect carriage, and if her shoulders are not well thrown back, the chances are that the effect of a square shawl will be anything but pleasing. If the lady stoops, or is at all round-shouldered, the shawl will have the effect of a window that has been cracked by a stone--it will look starred – it will not be smooth and even, but will present the appearance of lines radiating from the defective shoulders. For grace there is nothing like a scarf shawl, but only a few can, or know how to, wear it.

Under these circumstances a cloak or a mantle are safer. There is an infinite variety to choose from, but as the names and the fashion vary year by year it is useless to specify any. For the same reason, this constant change, it is best not to invest much capital in the purchase of one. Young people can wear smaller and shorter mantles than their elders, who require something larger and more imposing.

In winter there is nothing to compare to a seal skin; so much so that even an imitation is not to be despised. Velvets are ladylike, but they are expensive, and have not the durability of a seal skin. Velveteen cloaks are good and reasonable. Blue cloth or serge, braided with black, look well, and have been in favour for some time. We have seen a grey cloth cloak braided with black which has been much admired; also one of dark green cloth lined with grey, and, vice versa, of grey lined with green. For winter, the effect of lining a cloth cloak with another colour in good contrast is decidedly good. But everything depends upon the shape and cut of the cloak. It is the shape that tells far more than the material.

In France we find gloves and shoes have a prominent place among the accessories of a lady's toilette. To be '*bien chaussee et bien gantee*' is essential to being well dresseded. Good, well fitting gloves and shoes tell more than most other things among the French. At least a somewhat shabby and unpretending gown and bonnet, if accompanied by gloves that are of a good quality and colour and that fit well, and by shoes or boots that also fit well, and are of good style and make, will pass muster anywhere, while the reverse will fail.

It is remarkable that there is nothing which distinguishes a foreigner from an Englishwoman more than her gloves. They 'fit like a glove;' they are of a good colour, according well with the rest of the costume, neither too light nor too dark, but rather light than dark. There are no ends or corners of the fingers which are not well filled; there are no creases indicative of the gloves being of a wrong size, nor are they put on crooked with a twist given to the fingers, so that the seams of the glove do not appear straight. In short, a

Frenchwoman does not put on her glove anyhow as an Englishwoman does. To her it is a matter of great importance; to our country-woman it is a matter of indifference. We think the Frenchwoman right, because it is by what are called trifles that good and also great effects are produced.

We come now to an accessory of considerable importance – the hair. As a great amount of time is expended upon hair-dressing, and as no one ever thinks of wearing it in its natural state, and as nothing is more under the influence of fashion than the hair, it has become by consent of all an accessory of great importance. Will anyone affirm that it is a matter of indifference how the hair is dressed? Whether in plaits or bows? Whether in a crop, or twisted up in a coil? There is nothing which affects a lady's personal appearance more than the style in which she dresses her hair. We confess that we have a strong prejudice against a too submissive following of the fashion. Because in the first place we deny that fashion is always in the right, and in the second it rarely happens that the same style exactly suits two persons alike.

Nothing requires more consideration than the hair. It is one of a woman's greatest ornaments. We have high authority for saying this. Hair should always have the appearance of being well cared for. It should set off the shape of the head if it is good, and not aggravate any of its defects. A small head, well set on, is a great beauty. It tends more than anything else to that distinguished look which enhances all other beauty. Beauty, if accompanied by a look of refinement, is worth more than mere animal beauty, and nothing is more indicative of refinement and noble birth as a well-shaped head. It is the head which gives the impression of intellectual power. The well formed brow should not be demoralized by ringlets, which are suggestive only of a wax doll, nor should it be disfigured by being surmounted by a kind of cushion or roll of hair which gives the idea of weight and size. Nor should the hair have the appearance of a bird's nest, and look tumbled and untidy. This was lately the 'beau ideal' of a well dressed head. It was desired that it should appear unkempt and uncombed, as if it had been drawn through a quickset hedge. The back of the head, if well shaped, has a beautiful appearance, reminding one of a stag, which is so graceful in look and motion. But when it is disfigured by a large mass of hair, resembling a large pin-cushion, all that peculiar native grace which we so much admire is lost sight of. When all heads are made to look alike and equally large, there is no advantage in having a small and well shaped head. It seems as if the study of the present day were to make the head look large, and to conceal all its points. We miss the smooth braids of hair which set off the expanse of forehead, and the coils of plaits of hair, which ornamented, but did not conceal the back of the head. We miss the glossy look of the hair which indicated care, and prefer it infinitely to that which simulates neglect. It is perfectly true that one style does not suit all persons alike, any more than that the powder which was worn by our great-grandmothers was equally becoming to all. A low forehead, if the points of the brow are good, should have the hair drawn off it, whereas a high forehead which does not betoken any great intellectual power is disfigured by the same process. Smooth braids will not become a long face, nor puffs a broad one. A forehead which is already too high cannot bear to be heightened by coronets and cushions of hair, nor a countenance which indicates weakness to be made weaker still by limp luxurious curls. A stern face requires to be softened, while a weak one requires strength. The hair can generally do this. It depends upon how it is dressed.

They who are no longer young endeavour to impose upon the world by the use of wigs and fronts. These are an abomination, and in every instance they are easy of detection. There is something in the way in which false hair protests against the face and the face against it, which infallibly exposes it to be false. A lady with all the signs of years about her face makes her age the more apparent by the contrast of glossy dark hair which belongs to youth. Why is she afraid to wear her own grey hair? Grey hairs are no reproof, and we are quite sure they would harmonise better with the other marks of age than the wigs and fronts which prevail. There is something in the white hair of age which has a charm of its own. It is like the soft and mellow light of sunset. But unfortunately an old woman is not always inclined to accept the fact that she is old. She would rebel against it, but rebellion is useless. The fact remains the same. She is old notwithstanding her 'rouge' pot and her front, and she is growing older day by day.

Jewellery is another accessory. Jewels, real jewels, are in the possession of only a few. They are so costly that only millionaires or the heirs of heirlooms can have them. They are very beautiful, and have this one merit, that a few jewels, judiciously selected and worn, make a person well dressed at once. A diamond necklace and brooch, diamond earrings, and a few diamond stars glittering in the hair, will make almost a shabby dress pass muster at Court. But jewellery is a term that is applied to ornaments generally, and not to jewels only.

Sham jewellery is an abomination. It is a lie, and a pretension. At no time was so much sham jewellery made and worn. Every damsel has her brooches and her earrings. In nine cases out of ten they are mere trumpery, but, such as they are, no maid of all work will go out for her Sunday walk without her brooch and earrings and chain. She must have her locket too, fastened round her throat with black velvet, but it is all, with the exception of the velvet, a sham.

Ladies too have a weakness for sham jewellery. They will wear massive bracelets, cameo brooches of target dimensions, earrings, chains, all of what they pleasantly call French manufacture. It is called French in the shops in order to soften down its imposture, and to play upon the weakness of our country women who are apt to think that whatever is French must be good. But in many cases they are of Birmingham manufacture.

We enter our protest very strongly against the use of sham jewellery, though we must own without much hope of success, for, it must be admitted, that a great quantity of it is exceedingly pretty. We are not surprised that it should be popular, for who can resist the opportunity of making herself fine and 'beautiful for ever' at the cost of a few shillings, which is all that is necessary to lay in a fair stock of jewellery.

This sham jewellery is continually mistaken for real, so good is the resemblance.

If a duchess were to wear it everyone would take for granted that it was real, because she would not be supposed to wear anything that is unreal. We have heard of a lady who, possessing but very few jewels, always makes up for the deficiency by wearing sham diamonds. They are good of their kind, and no one ever suspects them to be false, simply because there is no reason why she should not have real diamonds, but, on the contrary, so far as the world knows, every reason why she should.

In the use of jewellery more than in anything else we maintain that all persons should dress according to their station and their means. If they can afford it, let them, but we recommend them not to act too much upon the old saying, that 'fine feathers make fine birds,' but to bear in mind that being well dressed means something more than well fitting, well selected clothes.

VI

'A FEW WORDS MORE'

It is very difficult, we might say impossible, to give any definite rules about dress. Fashions change so continually, that if we were to write a dissertation upon peplums, and trains, and gores, or give directions how to cut them out or make them, almost by the time this manual should come into circulation, they would have become portions of the past, and our hints would seem absurd and out of place. All that has seemed feasible to us we have done, which has been to give certain hints that the rocks upon which so many split, who make great endeavours to be well dressed, might be avoided by our readers.

There is no doubt that everyone wishes to dress well, whatever her means may be; and that no one thinks she dresses ill, whatever the world may think of her performance. We look at ourselves through coloured glass, and are apt to take the most favourable view of our own peculiarities:

O, wad some power the giftie gie us,
To see ourselves as others see us.

There are rules in dress, as there are in painting, which, if observed, will prevent our making 'frights' of ourselves. Anyone who starts for herself on a new line, and, throwing to the wind the received laws, adopts and carries out some crude theory of her own, however much she may entertain herself by her experiments, runs a great chance of making a figure of herself, and will infallibly obtain a reputation for conceit and affectation. No woman, unless she is a star of great magnitude, or a belle of note, can with impunity set at nought the received customs. She is by no means bound to follow fashion so implicitly and subserviently as to mar her own beauty. But a clever woman will always be able to avoid affronting fashion while she takes a line of her own. We use this phrase with a certain limitation, because if a woman were to take a line of her own unrestricted by certain 'convenances' of society and of fashion, she would certainly fall into the very error which we should be the first to declaim against, namely the error of eccentricity. A due regard for these 'convenances' will ensure that sense of propriety in dress which will make everyone remember both her station and her means. The fine lady will not effect the simplicity of the village girl, nor the village girl aspire to be mistaken for the fine lady. Both will maintain their own positions, and will be respected while they maintain them.

Let it also be borne in mind that a bonnet or cap, mantle or gown, may be very pretty in itself and very becoming to some persons, but not necessarily to everyone; generally to only a few. The young and the old have each their privileges. The one must not dress like the other. Though we have seen some who have been foolish enough to forget the years that have passed, and cannot realise the fact that they are no longer young, and vie with the youngest in the youthfulness of their attire, we do not, we admit, often find the young endeavouring to make themselves look older than they are. One who has thought much and written well on this subject says, 'Doubtless if there were any way of making old people young, either in looks or anything else, it would be a delightful invention; but meanwhile juvenile dressing is the last road we should recommend them to take.'

In conclusion, let every woman bear in mind that dress denotes character, that there is a symbolism in dress which they who have studied the matter can read without difficulty.

Toasts and Sentiments

AMATORY

British belles and British fashions.

Laughing lovers to merry maids.

Love and opportunity.

Love's slavery.

Love without licentiousness, and pleasure without excess.

Love, liberty, and length of blissful days.

Love without fear, and life without care.

Love for one.

Life, love, liberty, and true friendship.

Love in every breast, liberty in every heart, and learning in every head.

Love at liberty, and liberty in love.

Love: may it never make a wise man play the fool.

Artless love and disinterested friendship.

All that love can give, and sensibility enjoy.

A speedy union to every lad and lass.

Beauty's best companion – Modesty.

Beauty, innocence, and modest merit.

Beauty without affectation, and virtue without deceit.

Community of goods, unity of hearts, nobility of sentiment, and truth of feeling to the lovers of the fair sex.

Charms to strike the sight, and merit to win the heart.

Constancy in love, and sincerity in friendship.

Here's a health to the maid that is constant and kind,

Who to charms bright as Venus's adds Diana's mind.

I'll toast Britain's daughters – let all fill their glasses –

Whose beauty and virtue the whole world surpasses.

May blessings attend them, go wherever they will,

And foul fall the man that e'er offers them ill.

Love without deceit, and matrimony without regret.

Love's garlands: may they ever entwine the brows of every true-hearted
lover.

Lovely woman – man's best and dearest gift of life.

Love to one, friendship to a few, and good-will to all.

Long life, pure love, and boundless liberty.

May love and reason be friends, and beauty and prudence marry.

May the lovers of the fair sex never want the means to defend them.

May the sparks of love brighten into a flame.

May the joys of the fair give pleasure to the heart.

May we be loved by those whom we love.

May we kiss whom we please, and please whom we kiss.

May the bud of affection be ripened by the sunshine of sincerity.

May a virtuous offspring succeed to mutual and honourable love.

May the presence of the fair curb the licentious.

May the confidence of love be rewarded with constancy in its object.

May the honourable lover attain the object of his wishes.

May the lovers of the fair be modest, faithful, and kind.

May the wings of love never lose a feather.

May the blush of conscious innocence ever deck the faces of the
British fair.

May the union of persons always be founded on that of hearts.

May the generous heart ever meet a chaste mate.

May the temper of our wives be suited to those of their husbands.

May true passion never meet with a slight.

May every woman have a protector, but not a tyrant.

BACCHANALIAN

May we act with reason when the bottle circulates.

May good fortune resemble the bottle and bowl,

And stand by the man who can't stand by himself.

May we never want wine, nor a friend to partake of it.

May our love of the glass never make us forget decency.

May the juice of the grape enliven each soul,

And good humour preside at the head of each bowl.

May mirth exalt the feast.

May we always get mellow with good wine.

May the moments of mirth be regulated by the dial of reason.

Champagne to our real friends, and real pain to our sham friends.

Come, every man now give his toast

Fill up the glass – I'll tell you mine:

Wine is the mistress I love most!

This is my toast – now give me thine.

Cheerfulness in our cups, content in our minds, and competency in our pockets.

Come, fill the glass and drain the bowl:

May Love and Bacchus still agree;

And every Briton warm his soul

With Cupid, Wine, and Liberty.

Good-humour: and may it ever smile at our board.

Full bags, a fresh bottle, and a beauty.

Good wine and good company to the lovers of reasonable enjoyment.

A friend and a bottle to give him.

A hearty supper, a good bottle, and a soft bed to every man who fights the battles of his country.

A full purse, a fresh bottle, and beautiful face.

A full bottle and a friend to partake of it.

A drop of good stuff and a snug social party,

To spend a dull evening, gay, social, and hearty.

A mirth-inspiring bowl.

A full belly, a heavy purse, and a light heart.

A bottle at night and business in the morning.

Beauty, wit, and wine.

Clean glasses and old corks.

Wine: may it be our spur as we ride over the bad roads of life

While we enjoy ourselves over the bottle, may we never drive prudence out of the room.

Wine – for there's no medicine like it.

Wine – the parent of friendship, composer of strife,

The soother of sorrow, the blessing of life.

Wine: the bond that cements the warm heart to a friend.

COMIC

May the tax-gatherer be forgiven in another world.

To the early bird that catches the worm.

To the bird in the hand that is worth two in the bush.

Our native land: may we never be lawfully sent out of it.

Sound hearts, sound sovereigns, and sound dispositions.

The Queen, and may true Britons never be without her likeness in their pockets.

The land we live in: may he who doesn't like it leave it.

The three great Generals in power - General Peace, General Plenty, and General Satisfaction.

The Bank of England's passport to travel with, and the Queen's picture for a companion.

May the parched pea never jump out of the frying-pan into the fire.

The three R's: Reading,'Riting, and 'Rithmetic.

May evil communications never corrupt good manners.

May the celebrated pin a day, of which we have heard so much, always make the groat a year.

May the groat a year never be unwisely invested in a Joint-Stock Company.

May that man never grow fat

Who carries two faces under one hat.

Here's to the best physicians – Dr Diet, Dr Quiet, and Dr Merryman.

Here's to the feast that has plenty of meat and very little table-cloth.

Here's to the full purse that never lacks friends.

May fools make feasts, and wise men eat them.

Here's to the man who never lets his tongue cut his own throat.

Here's to the man who never quarrels with his bread and butter.

Here's to the man who never looks a gift-horse in the mouth.

Here's to the old bird that is not to be caught with chaff.

CONSERVATIVE

A health to those ladies who set the example of wearing British productions.

May Her Majesty's Ministers ever have wisdom to plan our institutions, and energy and firmness to support them.

Confusion to all demagogues.

May the productions of Britain's isle never be invaded by foreigners.

May the throne and the altar never want standing armies to back them.

Our old nobility.

The man who builds up rather than he who pulls down.

The loyal adherents of the Queen and the true friends of the people.

The equilibrium of State, may it always be preserved.

The ancient ways.

Judicious reforms and reformers.

The universal advancement of the arts and sciences.

All our independent nobles and noble hearts.

May the dispensers of justice ever be impartial.

May French principles never corrupt English manners.

May the interests of the monarch and monarchy never be thought distinct.

May the worth of the nation be ever inestimable.

May taxation be lessened annually.

May the Gallic cock be always clipped by British valour if he crows too loud.

May the sword of justice be swayed by the hand of mercy.

May the seeds of dissension never find growth in the soil of Great Britain.

May the love of country be imprinted in every Briton's breast.

May our statesmen ever possess the justice of a More and the wisdom of a Bacon.

Queen and Country.

Liberty, not licence.

Confusion to all men who desert their party.

Party ties before all other ties.

The Queen: may she outlive her Ministers, and may they live long.

A lasting cement to all contending powers.

The protectors of commerce and the promoters of charity.

A revision of the code of criminal laws.

The Bar, the Pulpit, and the Throne.

GASTRONOMIC

Old England's roast beef: may it ever be the standing dish of Britons.

Our constitutional friends – the Baron and the Sir-loin.

Roast beef: may it always ennoble our veins and enrich our blood.

The roast beef of old England.

The Union dish: English beef, Scotch kale, and Irish potatoes.

ENGLISH

England, home, and beauty.

English oak and British valour.

England for ever: the land we live in.

England, Scotland, and Ireland: may their union remain undisturbed by plots or treachery to the end of time.

England, the queen of the isles and the queen of the main.

May old England's sons, the Americans, never forget their mother.

IRISH

A high toast to the enemies of Ould Ireland, Erin, the land of the brave and the bold.

Ireland; sympathy for her wrongs, and a determination to redress them.

The country that gave St Patrick birth, the birthplace of wit, and hospitality's home – dear Ould Ireland.

May Great Britain and Ireland be ever equally distinguished by their love of liberty and true patriotism.

May the enemies of Great Britain and Ireland never meet a friend in either country.

Justice to Ireland.

Ireland, Scotland, and England: may their union be happier than it has been.

SCOTCH

A health to the friends of Caledonia.

Caledonia, the nursery of learning and the birthplace of heroes.

Scotland and the productions of its soil.

Scottish heroes, and may their fame live for ever.

Scotland, the birthplace of valour, the country of worth.

The Queen and the Scottish Union.

The nobles of Caledonia and their ladies.

To the memory of Scottish heroines.

The Rose, Thistle, and Shamrock: may they flourish by the common graft of union.

To the memory of Scotland's heroes.

To the memory of those who have gloriously fallen in the noble struggle for independence.

LIBERAL

Annihilation to the trade of corruption.

An Englishman's birthright: trial by jury.

Addition to our trade, multiplication to our manufactures, subtraction to taxes, and reduction to places and pensions.

All the honest reformers of our country.

Britain: may the land of our nativity ever be the abode of freedom, and the birthplace of heroes.

Britain's annals: may they never suffer a moral or political blot.

Confusion to those who barter the cause of their country for sordid gain.

Confusion to those who, wearing the mask of patriotism, pull it off and desert the cause of liberty in the hour of trial.

Confusion to those despots who combine against the liberties of mankind.

Disappointment to all those who form expectations of places and pensions on the ruin of their country.

Everlasting life to the man who gave the death-blow to the slave trade.

Community, unity, navigation, and trade.

Faith in every kind of commerce.

Freedom to the oppressed, and slavery to the oppressors.

Freedom to all who dare contend for it.

Oblivion to all party rage.

Humanity to all created beings, especially to our own species, whether black or white.

No party except mankind.

May the meanest Briton scorn the highest slave.

Old England: and may those who ill-use her be speedily kicked off.

May Great Britain and Ireland be ever equally distinguished by their love of liberty and true patriotism.

May every succeeding century maintain the principles of the glorious Revolution, enjoy the blessings of them, and transmit them to future ages unimpaired and improved.

May the whole universe be incorporated in one city, and every inhabitant presented with the freedom.

May Britons share the triumphs of freedom, and ever contend for the rights and liberties of mankind.

May freedom's fire take new birth at the grave of liberty.

May our country be, as it has ever been, a secure asylum to the unfortunate and oppressed.

High wages, and sense to keep them.

May the freedom of election be preserved, the trial by jury maintained, and the liberty of the press secured to the latest posterity.

May the tree of liberty flourish round the globe, and every human being partake of the fruits.

May truth and liberty prevail throughout the world.

May all partial and impolitic taxes be abolished.

May Britons never have a tyrant to oppose either in Church or State.

May the sons of liberty marry the daughters of virtue.

May Britons never suffer invasion, nor invade the rights of others.

May the miseries of war be banished from all enlightened nations.

May our trade and manufactures be unrestrained by the fetters of monopoly.

May the whole world become more enlightened and civilised.

May revolutions never cease while tyranny exists.

Our constitution as settled at the Revolution.

May the people of England always oppose a bad Ministry, and give vigour to a good one.

The British Lion: may he never rise in anger nor lie down in fear.

The majesty of the people of England.

The memory of our brave ancestors who brought about the
Revolution, and may a similar spirit actuate their descendants.

The sacred decree of heaven – Let all mankind be free.

The British Constitution; and confusion to those who dislike it.

The people – the only source of legitimate power.

The subject of liberty and the liberty of the subject.

The non-electors of Great Britain: may they speedily be enfranchised.

The greatest happiness of the greatest number.

May the nation that plots against another's liberty or prosperity fall a
victim to its own intrigues.

LITERARY

Toleration and liberty of the press.

The Fourth Estate.

The liberty of the press, and success to its defenders.

The Press: the great bulwark of our liberties, and may it ever remain
unshackled.

The glorious literature of Scotland.

The glorious literature of Ireland.

The glorious literature of England.

LOYAL

Queen Victoria: and may her royal offspring adorn the position they are
destined to fill.

All the royal family.

A speedy export to all the enemies of Britain without a drawback.

A lasting peace or an honourable war.

A health to our English patriots.

Agriculture and its improvers.

All the societies associated for promoting the happiness of the human
race.

All the charitable institutions of Great Britain.

An Englishman's castle – his house: may it stand for ever.

Britons in unity, and unity in Britain.

British virtue: may it always find a protector, but never need one.

Great Britain's rising star: the Prince of Wales.

Holy pastors, honest magistrates, and humane rulers.

Improvement to the inventions of our country.

Improvement to our arts, and invention to our artists.

May the sword of Justice be swayed by the hand of Mercy.

May the love of country always prevail.

May St George's Channel be the only difference ever known between England and Ireland.

May the eagles of the Continent never build their nests in this little island.

May British valour shine when every other light is out.

May Britons, when they do strike, strike home.

May the populace of our country be remarkable for their loyalty and domestic happiness.

May our sons be honest and fair, and our daughters modest and fair.

May every Briton's hand be ever hostile to tyranny.

May the annals of Great Britain's history be unstained with crime and unpolluted With bloody deeds.

May our jurors ever possess sufficient courage to uphold their verdict.

May every Briton manfully withstand corruption.

May we never be afraid to die for our country.

Our wives, homes, country, and Queen.

May the health of our sovereign keep pace with the wishes of her people.

May every Briton manfully withstand tyranny.

May the glory of Britain never cease to shine.

May the honours of our nobility be without stain.

May Britons be invincible by united force.

May the olive of peace renovate the sinking fund of the British nation.

May the throne and the altar never want standing armies to back them.

May Britons secure their conquests by clemency.

May we as citizens be free without faction, and as subjects loyal without servility.

May loyalty flourish for ever.

May liberty ever find an altar in Britain surrounded by devoted worshippers.

May the British bull never be cowed.

May our hearts ever be possessed with the love of country.

May the British soil alone produce freedom's sons.

May the brave never want protection.

May sovereigns and subjects reign in each other's hearts by love.

May we ever honestly uphold our rights.

May we never cease to deserve well of country.

May Britons ever defend, with bold unflinching hand, Their throne,
    their altar, and their native land.

May the liberties of the people be immortal.

May the heart of an Englishman ever be Liberty Hall.

May the brow of the brave be adorned by the hand of beauty.

May we never find danger lurking on the borders of security.

May the laurels of Great Britain never be blighted.

May all mankind make free to enjoy the blessings of liberty, but never
    take the liberty to subvert the principles of freedom.

May Britannia's hand ever be armed with the bolts of Jove.

May the ensign of loyalty float over us – the jack of pure patriotism
    lead us--and may the pendant of every British man-of-war serve as a
    cat-o-nine-tails to whip our enemies with.

May England's name and England's fame stand for ever pure, great and
    free.

May every true Briton be possessed of peace, plenty, and content.

May every Briton leave his native land at honour's call,

To fight, to conquer, or, like Wolfe, to fall.

May every Briton act the patriot's part.

May victory spin the robe of glory for the brave, and fame enrol his deeds.

May the laws never be misconstrued.

May the weight of our taxes never bend the back of our credit.

May increasing success crown the island of traders,

And its shores prove the grave of all foreign invaders.

MASONIC

May every worthy brother who is willing to work and labour through
    the day, be happy at night with his friend, his love, and a cheerful
    glass.

May all freemasons be enabled to act in a strict conformity to the rules of their order.

May our actions as masons be properly squared.

May masonry flourish until nature expire,

And its glories ne'er fade till the world is on fire.

The female friends of freemasons.

May the brethren of our glorious craft be ever distinguished in the world by their regular lives; more than by their gloves and aprons.

May concord, peace; and harmony subsist in all regular lodges, and always distinguish freemasons.

May masonry prove as universal as it is honourable and useful.

May every brother learn to live within the compass, and watch upon the square.

May the lodges in this place be distinguished for love, peace, and harmony.

All noblemen and right worshipful brothers who have been grand masters.

May peace, harmony, and concord subsist among freemasons, and may every idle dispute and frivolous distinction be buried in oblivion.

All regular lodges.

All the friends of the craft.

As we meet upon the level, may we part upon the square.

All faithful and true brothers.

All brothers who have been grand masters.

Every brother who keeps the key of knowledge from intruders, but cheerfully gives it to a worthy brother.

Every brother who maintains a consistency in love and sincerity in friendship.

Every worthy brother who was at first duly prepared, and whose heart still retains an awful regard to the three great lights of masonry.

Golden eggs to every brother, and goldfinches to our lodges.

Honour and influence to every public-spirited brother.

All freeborn sons of the ancient and honourable craft.

May the square, plumb-line, and level regulate the conduct of every brother.

May the morning have no occasion to censure the night spent by freemasons.

May the hearts of freemasons agree, although their heads should differ.

May every mason participate in the happiness of a brother.

May every brother have a heart to feel and a hand to give.

May discord, party rage, and insolence be for ever rooted out from among masons.

May covetous cares be unknown to freemasons.

May all freemasons go hand in hand in the road of virtue.

May we be more ready to correct our own faults than to publish the errors of a brother.

May the prospect of riches never induce a mason to do that which is repugnant to virtue.

May unity and love be ever stamped upon the mason's mind.

May no freemason desire plenty but with the benevolent view to relieve the indigent.

May no freemason wish for more liberty than constitutes happiness, nor more freedom than tends to the public good.

May the deformity of vice in other men teach a mason to abhor it in himself.

May the cares which haunt the heart of the covetous be unknown to the freemason.

Prosperity to masons and masonry

Relief to all indigent brethren.

To the secret and silent.

The great lodge of England.

The great lodge of Scotland.

To the memory of him who first planted the vine.

To the perpetual honour of freemasons.

The masters and wardens of all regular lodges.

To all masons who walk by the line.

To the memory of the Tyrian artist.

May all freemasons live in love and die in peace.

May love animate the heart of every mason.

May all freemasons ever taste and relish the sweets of freedom.

MILITARY

May our commanders have the eye of a Hawke and the heart of a Wolfe.

To the memory of Wellington and all like him.

Chelsea Hospital and its supporters.

To the memory of Sir Thomas Picton, and all our brave countrymen who fell at Waterloo.

May every British officer possess Wolfe's conduct and courage, but not meet with his fate.

May the enemy's flag be surmounted by the British standard.

May the arms borne by a soldier never be used in a bad cause.

May British soldiers fight to protect, and conquer to save.

May the gifts of fortune never cause us to steer out of our latitude.

May the brow of the brave never want a wreath of laurel to adorn it.

May the army of Great Britain never feel dismayed at its enemies.

May the brave soldier who never turned his back to the enemy never have a friend turn his back to him.

May bronze and medals not be the only reward of the brave.

May no rotten members infect the whole corps.

May the laurels of Great Britain never be blighted.

May all weapons of war be used for warlike purposes only.

May the soldier never fall a sacrifice but to glory.

To the memory of Sir John Moore, and all the brave fellows who fell with him in the action of Corunna; and may their gallant conduct stimulate every British soldier in the hour of danger.

To the memory of all brave soldiers who fall in defence of their country.

The memory of a great general and splendid genius, though ambitious and tyrannic – Napoleon Bonaparte.

NAVAL

May our iron-clads do as much as out-brave old oaks.

May John Bull ever be commander-in-chief of the ocean.

May Old England, a world within herself, reign safe for ever in her floating towers.

To the memory of Nelson, and all like him.

Greenwich Hospital and its supporters.

May every British seaman fight bravely and be rewarded honourably.

May rudders govern and ships obey.

May no true son of Neptune ever flinch from his gun.

May no son of the ocean ever be devoured by his mother.

May our navy never know defeat but by name

May our sailors for ever prove lords of the main.

May the deeds never be forgot that were done at Trafalgar and
Waterloo.

May the cause of British liberty ever be defended by her hearts of oak.

May our officers and tars be valiant and brave.

Success to the fair for manning the navy.

May gales of prosperity waft us to the port of happiness.

May our seamen, from the captain to the cabin-boy, be like our ships,
hearts of oak.

More hard ships for Britain, and less to her enemies.

May the pilot of reason guide us to the harbour of rest.

May the memory of the noble Nelson inspire every seaman to do his
duty.

May the tar who loses one eye in defence of his country, never see distress
with the other.

Should the French come to Dover, may they mis-deal in their landing.

To Nelson's memory here's a health,

And to his gallant tars,

And, may our British seamen bold

Despise both wounds and scars;

Make France and Spain,

And all the main,

And all their foes to know,

Britons reign o'er the main

While the stormy winds do blow.

The British navy, the world's check-string.

The heart of a sailor: may it be like heart of oak.

Though our bold tars are fortune's sport, may they ever be fortune's
care.

The flag of England: may it ever brave the battle and the breeze.

The sea, the rough sea, the open sea: may our lives be spent upon it.

The sea, the sleepless guardian of the world.

The memory of Lord Howe and the glorious 1st of June.

Safe arrivals to our homeward and outward-bound fleets.

RELIGIOUS

The friends of religion, liberty, and science in every part of the globe.

The honest reformers of our laws and religion.

The clergy of the United Kingdom who have always supported the good cause: may they continue to do so.

The Pulpit, the Bar, and the Throne.

The friends of religious toleration, whether they are within or without the Establishment.

SENTIMENTAL

May we ever have a sufficiency for ourselves, and a trifle to spare for our friends.

May we always look forward to better times, but never be discontented with the present.

May the miseries of war never more have existence in the world.

May the wing of friendship never moult a feather.

May our artists never be forced into artifice to gain applause and fortune.

May solid honour soon take place of seeming religion.

May our thoughts never mislead our judgment.

May filial piety ever be the result of a religious education.

May real merit meet reward, and pretension its punishment.

May prosperity never make us arrogant, nor adversity mean.

May we live happy and die in peace with all mankind.

May the unsuspecting man never be deceived.

May noise and nonsense be ever banished from social company.

May the faults of our neighbours be dim and their virtues glaring.

May industry always be the favourite of Fortune.

May the rich be charitable and the poor grateful.

May the misfortunes of others be always examined at the chart of our own conduct.

May we never be so base as to envy the happiness of another.

May we live to learn, and learn to live well.

May we be more ready to correct our own faults than to publish the faults of others.

May we never hurt our neighbour's peace by the desire of appearing witty.

Modesty in our discourses, moderation in our wishes, and mutuality in our affections.

May we never envy those who are happy, but strive to imitate them.

May we derive amusement from business and improvement from pleasure.

May our faults be written on the sea-shore, and every good action prove a wave to wash them out.

May virtue find fortune always an attendant.

May we never repine at our condition, nor be depressed by poverty.

May reality strengthen the joys of imagination.

May we never make a sword of our tongue to wound a good man's reputation.

May our distinguishing mark be merit rather than money.

A total abolition of the slave trade.

A heart to glow for others' good.

A heart to feel and a heart to give.

A period to the sorrows of an ingenuous mind.

A health to our sweethearts, our friends, and our wives:

May fortune smile on them the rest of their lives.

May genius and merit never want a friend.

Adam's ale: and may so pure an element be always at hand.

All that gives us pleasure.

All our wants and wishes.

All our absent friends on land and sea.

An honest guide and a good pilot.

As we bind so may we find.

As we travel through life may we live well on the road.

May truth and liberty prevail throughout the world.

May we never engage in a bad cause, and never fly from a good one.

May domestic slavery be abolished throughout the world.

May the fruits of England's soil never be denied to her children.

SPORTING

May the lovers of the chase never want the comforts of life.

May every fox-hunter be well mounted.

May we always enjoy the pleasures of shootings and succeed with foul and fair.

The staunch hound that never spends tongue but where he ought.

The gallant huntsman that plunges into the deep in pursuit of his game.

The clear-sighted sportsman that sees his game with one eye.

The steady sportsman that always brings down his game.

The beagle that runs by nose and not by sight.

The jolly sportsman that never beats about the bush.

The huntsman's pleasures – the field in the morning and the bottle at night.

The joys of angling.

The jolly sportsman who enters the covert without being bit by the fox.

May the pleasures of sportsmen never know an end.

May the jolly fox-hunter never want freedom of soul nor liberality of heart.

May we always gain fresh vigour from the joys of the chase.

May the sportsman's day be spent in pleasure.

May strength the sportsman's nerves in vigour brace;

May cruelty ne'er stain with foul disgrace

The well-earned pleasures of the chase.

May the love of the chase never interrupt our attention of the welfare of the country.

May every sport prove as innocent as that of the field.

May the bows of all British bowmen be strong, their strings sound, and may their arrows fly straight to the mark.

May we always run the game breast high.

May those who love the crack of the whip never want a brush to pursue.

May the heart of a sportsman never know affliction but by name.

MISCELLANEOUS

The three A's:

    Abundance, abstinence, and annihilation.

    Abundance to the poor.

    Abstinence to the intemperate.

    Annihilation to the wicked.

The three B's:

    Bachelors, banns, and buns.

    Bachelors, for the maidens.

    Banns for the bachelors.

    Buns after the consummation of the banns.

The three C's:

    Cheerfulness, content, and competency.

    Cheerfulness in our cups.

    Content in our minds.

    Competency in our pockets.

The three F's:

    Firmness, freedom, and fortitude.

    Firmness in the senate.

    Freedom on the land.

    Fortitude on the waves.

The three F's:

    Friendship, feeling, and fidelity.

    Friendship without interest.

    Feeling to our enemies.

    Fidelity to our friends.

The three F's: Fat, fair, and forty.

The three generals in peace:

    General peace.

    General plenty.

    General satisfaction.

The three generals in power:

    General employment.

    General industry.

    General comfort.

The three H's:
    Health, honour, and happiness.
    Health to all the world.
    Honour to those who seek for it.
    Happiness in our homes.

The three L's:
    Love, life, and liberty.
    Love pure.
    Life long.
    Liberty boundless.

The three M's:
    Mirth, music, and moderation.
    Mirth at every board.
    Music in all instruments.
    Moderation in our desires.

The three golden balls of civilisation:
    Industry, commerce, and wealth.

The three companions of beauty:
    Modesty, love, and constancy.

The three blessings of this life:
    Health, wealth, and a good conscience.

The four comforts of this life:
    Love, liberty, health, and a contented mind.

The three spirits that have no souls:
    Brandy, rum, and gin.

The three L's;
    Love, loyalty, and length of days.

The three M's;
    Modesty, moderation, and mutuality.

Modesty in our discourse.
Moderation in our wishes.
Mutuality in our affection.

THE MUSICIAN'S TOAST

May a crotchet in the head never bar the utterance of good notes.
May the lovers of harmony never be in want of a note, and its enemies
die in a common chord.

THE SURGEON'S TOAST

The man that bleeds for his country.

THE WAITER'S TOAST

The clever waiter who puts the cork in first and the liquor afterwards.

THE GLAZIER'S TOAST

The praiseworthy glazier who takes panes to see his way through life.

THE GREENGROCER'S TOAST

May we spring up like vegetables, have turnip noses, radish cheeks, and
carroty hair; and may our hearts never be hard like those of cab-
bages, nor may we be rotten at the core.

THE PAINTER'S TOAST

When we work in the wet may we never want for driers.

THE TALLOW CHANDLER'S TOAST

May we make light of our misfortunes, melt the fair when we press them, and make our foes wax warm in our favour.

THE HATTER'S TOAST

When the rogue naps it, may the lesson be felt.

THE TAILOR'S TOAST

May we always sheer out of a lawsuit, and by so doing cut bad company.

THE BAKER'S TOAST

May we never be done so much as to make us crusty.

THE LAWYER'S TOAST

May the depth of our potations never cause us to let judgment go by default.

LATIN

Ad finem esto fidelis.
Be faithful to the end.

Amor patriae.
The love of our country.

Dilige amicos.
Love your friends.

Dum vivimus vivamus.
Let us live while we live.

Esto perpetua.
Be thou perpetual.

Palmam qid meruit ferate.
Let him who has won bear the palm.

Pro aris et focis.
For our altars and fireside.

Vox populi vox Dei.
The voice of the people is the voice of God.

THE END

If you are interested in purchasing other books published by Tempus,
or in case you have difficulty finding any Tempus books in your local bookshop,
you can also place orders directly through our website

www.tempus-publishing.com